HOW TO COLLECT:
A COMPLETE GUIDE

HOW TO COLLECT: A COMPLETE GUIDE

The Art of Buying,
Displaying, Preserving, Protecting,
& Selling Your Antiques

Carole G. Rogers

E. P. Dutton ◆ New York

Published in the United States by Elsevier-Dutton Publishing Co., Inc., 2 Park Avenue, New York, N.Y. 10016

Library of Congress Catalog Card Number: 79-53335

ISBN: 0-525-93190-2 (cloth)
ISBN: 0-525-47671-7 (paper)

Published simultaneously in Canada by Clarke, Irwin & Company Limited, Toronto and Vancouver

Designed by Barbara Cohen

10 9 8 7 6 5 4 3 2 1

First Edition

20663 ✓

CONTENTS

HOW TO COLLECT:
A COMPLETE GUIDE

WHY COLLECT?

Why collect? To anyone who is already addicted the question might more appropriately be asked: Why not collect? Pastime becomes passion so quickly that our enthusiasm obscures our perspective. We are not the first—or even the hundredth—generation of collectors. "The urge to collect is as old as man himself," Aline Saarinen reminds us in *The Proud Possessors.*

Although the impulse to collect has always been a part of human history, the reasons people collect have changed. Among the earliest civilizations, curiosity—an effort to make some sense out of one's environment—was a major motive. A study made by two French paleontologists reveals that even in the Paleolithic or Old Stone Age men collected fossils. Superstition—the desire to protect oneself from harm—was another reason. If one amulet brought good fortune, then surely ten would bring even more.

Certain ages and certain societies encouraged collectors more than others. In periods of prosperity collecting flourished. During the Roman Empire the fever ran so high that almost everyone, including such famous citizens as Brutus, Cassius, Cicero, and Julius Caesar, collected something: sculpture, coins, fine books, silver. The Japanese aristocracy amassed impressive collections during the eighth century A.D., which has been called "the blossom time" of Japanese culture. And so did the Chinese emperors during the Sung dynasty (A.D. 960–1279). In the West the Renaissance marks a high point in the history of collecting.

Whatever the age or the country, it has usually been the wealthy collectors—the Chinese emperor Hui Tsung, the Medici, Madame de Pompadour, J. P. Morgan—whom history remembers. For these men and women pursuing their passion was not a problem. They had both time and money. They collected in a grand style.

But, particularly in later centuries, they were not the only ones to respond to the beautiful or the bizarre, the old or the rare. Jules Fleury-Husson, a nineteenth-century French writer who was also associated with the ceramics factory and museum in Sèvres, was a shrewd observer of the social scene. He was not speaking only to kings and queens when he described the path to becoming a true collector: "Do not occupy yourself with politics; never go to the theater; forbid yourself to open a book; scorn the pleasures of family; always have ready money in your pocket." In the United States John Spargo, an authority on American pottery, observed in 1926 in *Early American Pottery and China* that the collector of modest means is the only one entitled to respect.

Although Spargo would no doubt be horrified at what a modest collector must now spend to pursue this passion, he would probably be delighted to learn how many such collectors there are today.

The evidence can be gathered from many sources.

◆ In the United States dealers account for the bulk of antiques and collectibles sold. It is not easy to measure such sales, but one clue can be gleaned from the amount of advertising in trade magazines and newspapers. During the first six months of 1979 dealers increased their advertising budgets by more than half a million dollars.

◆ The auction market is booming. In the United States alone during the 1978/79 season sales increased forty percent over the previous year's totals.

◆ New antiques magazines and newspapers continue to appear and prosper. *Art and Antiques* began in July 1978 and had reached a circulation of 50,000 by the end of 1979. *Antiques World* published its first issue in November 1978 and twelve months later had a circulation of 41,000 and more than 600 advertising pages for the year.

◆ The number of antiques shows and flea markets is increasing at an amazing rate. Collectaholics can find a show somewhere every day of the year, except perhaps for the major religious holidays. In peak seasons, such as late spring and early autumn, the choice of weekend events is staggering. For anybody who attends one of these shows or markets, the crowds alone are powerful evidence that more and more people consider themselves collectors.

All of this increased activity brings up several questions.

1. *Who are these collectors?* They are both young and old, male and female. They include every ethnic background and every region of the country. They live in high-rise apartments, in suburban split-levels, on farms. In other words, today's collectors can be found everywhere. The epidemic is so widespread that one collector's magazine wryly reported that groups of Collectors Anonymous are now forming around the country, where trained personnel help sufferers "kick the habit" and cure themselves of the dread malady.

2. *What are they collecting?* In a word, everything. Dealers, auctioneers, and museum curators agree that collectors are enthusiastic about so many different kinds of items that it almost defies description.

In general, the demand for antiques and collectibles seems to have lowered the age at which objects become acceptable. Few antiques shows could survive if items more than 100 years old were the only ones allowed. And so, while interest in eighteenth-century furniture, Ming dynasty porcelain, and Regency silver grows, so does interest in Mission oak furniture, art pottery, and Depression glass.

Combine a list of broad categories, such as miniatures, commemoratives, limited editions, ephemera, and industrial memorabilia with specific items such as dolls, toys, tools, clocks, quilts, and pipes and you still do not in any way capture the diversity, imagination, and tenacity of today's collector. A West Virginia collector specializes in antique mousetraps—the kind that catches the mouse alive. An Ohio collector has accumulated more than 650 Cracker Jack prizes.

Some collectors are attracted to the works of one artist or craftsman: a Revere, a Tiffany, a Hitchcock. Others prefer to specialize in a particular kind of material: wood, perhaps, or textiles or glass. And within each of these specialties there are dozens of subspecialties. As an example, take a look at some of the varieties of glass collections. Obvious subdivisions—blown glass, pattern glass, cut glass, Depression glass, cameo glass, carnival glass—come to mind most quickly. Then there are collections of bottles, vases, compotes, decanters, plates, and lamps; candy containers, candlesticks, bells, and paperweights. There are collections of cranberry, ruby, Peachblow, Vaseline, and milk glass. There is early American, Victorian, Art Nouveau, and Art Deco. There is Heisey, Sandwich, Fenton, Cambridge, Tiffany, and Steuben; Waterford, Val St. Lambert, and Lalique. The point is not in the completeness of the listing but in the diversity.

3. The final question—*Why are they collecting?*—has no single answer either. Observers who tend toward psychological explanations suggest that the urge to collect may be an expression of self-identity or a sublimation of sexual desires or perhaps a harmless outlet for a craving for power. Others, who enjoy looking for sociological trends, believe that the current surge in collecting betrays our sense of being adrift without a sense of the past. It is thus a part of our search for our roots, a nostalgic journey into the past, an attempt to come to terms with our disposable present by preserving some of yesterday's artifacts.

While there may be some truth in those insights, there are other less introspective reasons for the collecting mania that grips us. The average person has both more time and more money to devote to a hobby. Increased leisure time has expanded people's horizons. Books, television, magazines, even adult-education courses have introduced more and more people to the worlds of art and history. People travel farther from home; they visit museums and historic sites more frequently. But collecting is not only an educational experience, it is also a social one. It's fun. And many collectors discover as they pursue their hobby that fellow collectors become their closest friends. Finally, there are the financial reasons. In inflationary times such as the 1970s were, people tend to become disenchanted with investments such as stocks and bonds and turn to more tangible items in an effort to keep pace with inflation.

Almost everyone has a favorite "gee whiz" story: the painting bought at a flea market for $100 and later appraised at $10,000; the mechanical bank bought for $150 and sold for $1500; the highboy bought in 1970 for $5000 and sold in 1978 for $21,000. The stories sound fantastic, but a good percentage of them are true. There is truth enough, anyway, to spread today's collecting fever.

These days the appeal of collecting is so universal that for every established collector there are dozens more just taking their first steps in the field. This book is meant for anyone who feels the tug of collecting, who wants to buy antiques or collectibles for almost any reason—for their beauty, historical significance, humor, rarity, or investment value; for one's own enjoyment or profit.

BEGINNING AT THE BEGINNING

It is popular these days to speak of goals—in careers, in life. Even in the earliest stages of collecting it is wise to consider the ultimate destination of the path you choose. Collectors who do so can expect the same benefits as a businessman who makes a five-year plan.

Deciding where you are going helps you make decisions along the way. At first you may have only a vague idea of what you'd like to do. But that shouldn't stop you from setting your goals, you can always adjust them later. In fact, you will have to as you learn more, as the market changes, and so forth. The important thing is to give some thought to why you're collecting. If, for example, your primary interest is to decorate your home with rare, valuable, or unusual objects that will make your home unique, you will want to apply certain tests to each object as you buy. Is the piece you want aesthetically pleasing? Does it have a vitality of its own? Is it appropriate for your home? Partners' desks and Wooton desks are both highly collectible, but few homes can show them to advantage. One decorator suggests that you should not buy anything unless you can think of at least two different places you can use it. Another suggests that it's good to start with basic pieces, such as tables, chairs, or lamps, that take the place of modern versions and often cost less than modern versions. You therefore incur less risk, but you are still taking steps toward the "look" you want.

If you choose instead to try to form a collection, there are other questions to ask yourself. Do you like to finish the things you start? Would you enjoy acquiring all the varieties of a certain object? Would you prefer to put things together in a way that has never been done before?

Make a personal statement with your collection? Or add something to the knowledge of a field? A collection reveals a great deal about the collector. Your taste, your imagination, your persistence, even your philosophy of life will be on display.

Sir Kenneth Clark, the British writer and art historian, has observed that there are two kinds of collectors: those who want to complete a series and those who simply respond to the things that bewitch them. Whichever course appeals to you, there is a variety of levels in both price and quality.

Traditionally, a series collector indulged in coins, stamps, or perhaps old books. Today's series collectors have a wider range from which to choose. Limited editions are designed to appeal to them; there is satisfaction, even a thrill, in acquiring every Bing and Grondahl Christmas plate. Unfortunately, the rapidly expanding market in "limited editions" exploits that appeal. Although the prices are generally reasonable and the pieces accessible, the quality is uneven and rarity often a very questionable matter.

Clark's second category—those who respond to a broad range of objects—includes those who decorate their homes with a mixture of antiques or collectibles. In its extreme form this can mean a Benjamin Sonnenberg, who filled a thirty-seven-room New York town house with marvelous art, furniture, brass, silver, and other antiques.

It means those whose collections stand as a tribute to one man's or one woman's taste. An Abby Aldrich Rockefeller or a Stewart Gregory, for example, whose folk art collections were extraordinary. But it also includes the many thousands of modest collectors who arm themselves with aesthetic principles and historical information, add their personal intuition, and acquire impressive collections in any number of specialized fields.

One museum curator makes a valuable distinction between an acquirer and a collector. He is both, he adds quickly, but he does not make the mistake of confusing the two. An acquirer buys without thought, responding to whim and without finding out much about what he is buying. A collector, on the other hand, takes his passion for things one step further. He takes the time to learn about his field, makes careful choices, and has established standards, priorities, and an ultimate destination for his collection.

An auctioneer offers another perspective on the same point when describing a collection of cut glass he was asked to appraise. He was disap-
pointed to find not a collection, but merely an accumulation of pieces.
There was little of value, he says. The collector had not made an effort
to apply any aesthetic standards, had not searched out the fine, the rare,
the extraordinary.

On the other hand, a collection of extraordinary objects can enhance
the value of each individual item forever afterward. A collector of mechanical banks will point proudly to a bank that had been in the John
Meyer collection. A collector of decoys will describe one of his favorite
items as being from the famous William Mackey collection.

After you have determined your goal, you can begin to zero in on a
target area. Ask any expert in the field of collecting—auctioneer, dealer,
museum curator—what fields would be good for a beginner, and the answers are not encouraging. There is, they say, hardly a field that hasn't
seen great surges of activity in recent years. Prices are going up. Bargains
are harder to find. Whatever field you choose you'll be competing with
experts and collectors who seem to have no limits to their budgets. That
is true. However, such advice should not deter you. There are good
things to collect and ways to begin.

In the beginning make your task easier rather than harder: choose a
wide range for your collection. If you choose porcelain, for instance, you
might decide to specialize in Royal Worcester because you like their
glazes. Royal Worcester dates from 1862 but is still being manufactured
today. Gradually, as you become familiar with the field, you might
move along to old Worcester, dating from 1783 to 1862, and finally to
Dr. Wall Worcester, a specialty that narrows your focus to the period
between 1751 and 1783, at the outside, and puts you in a high-price category, one where mistakes cannot be taken lightly.

Will you look for a relatively unresearched area, one with little background material available? If so, you will have to do much of the
groundwork yourself: decide for yourself what is quality and what is
not, what is a good price and what is not, what is genuine and what is
not. Down this route lie challenging research, many risks, and quite
possibly lower prices. Once an antique or collectible becomes the subject of a book or of a major museum exhibition, it often becomes more

available, but usually at a higher price and with greater competition among buyers.

If, on the other hand, you choose a well-marked field, you will find background material readily available. It is likely that others will already have established the guidelines for quality and rarity; prices will be higher and less flexible, perhaps even collected in a price guide. There will be more competition for quality items. And there will be more companionship, too. Many popular fields of collecting have clubs, and members in search of similar objects become good friends.

Once you have thought a bit about these areas, take a walk through several antiques shops or visit some shows. Get an idea of what is available in your area, what is popular, what suits your tastes and your budget. You may then come up with a target area. (All of this becomes quite academic, of course, if you've been wandering through antiques shops for years and are already hooked on Jumeau dolls or Regina music boxes.)

When you know *why* you're buying and, in general, *what* you're buying, you can establish a set of criteria for your purchases.

The most important advice for new collectors to remember is twofold. First, *buy what you like.* Established collectors may say it in a variety of ways. "There is an element of love involved in forming a collection." Or "I only buy something that speaks to me." But the message is the same. It's important to know, as quickly as possible, what is worthwhile in your field and what is not. If you're buying what you like, it isn't a chore to spend the time it takes to learn the difference between the good and the ordinary.

Second, *buy quality*—the best you can afford. This is important, no matter what your field. Everyone loves a bargain, and the temptation to buy cheap is almost irresistible. But, in the long run, a fine collection cannot be based primarily on bargains. Try always to buy one good piece instead of two lesser ones. Good pieces generally have more aesthetic vitality, more historical significance, and ultimately more value than second-rate pieces. Advanced collectors usually move on to purchasing only great pieces, where the rewards are also greater. The strength of the auction market at top price levels bears witness to this trend. *Trading up,* as it's called, is evident in almost every field of collecting.

If quality becomes your criterion because quality itself gives you plea-

sure, then your other objectives, such as creating a charming environment for your home, shedding new light on the works of a particular
craftsman, or keeping up with inflation, will also be reached.

This is perhaps a good place to pause and consider antiques and collectibles as investments. In an inflationary age such as ours, few people
are so wealthy that they need not care what happens to their money.
And although you may not buy antiques or collectibles simply for their resale value, it is a fact that the money you spend on a collection is money
that's not available for other uses: money that's not earning interest in
a savings account or invested in a money-market fund. And so today's collector, especially the one on a budget, cannot totally ignore the question
of value. On the other hand, *it is absolutely imperative to remember that
the collector who acquires objects solely for profit often loses on the transaction.*
The spectacular profits some collectors have made in recent years obscure two important facts: First, in most cases, the value of the antique
or collectible must appreciate fast enough to cover not only the rate of
inflation but also the costs inherent in keeping and protecting the item.
A stock certificate can be kept quite cheaply and safely in a broker's safe;
a Chinese vase is somewhat more of a problem. And remember, too,
that vases don't pay dividends. Second, antiques and collectibles are not
liquid; that is, they cannot always be sold quickly and easily. You must
be willing to tie up your money for the long term.

Investing in antiques is a high-risk business, a fact that may actually
increase its appeal to some people. But it is no easy matter to show a
profit in today's market. The classic areas of collecting—fine furniture,
Oriental rugs, porcelain—*have* shown excellent price increases. But in
recent years they have sometimes been overshadowed by offbeat items:
weathervanes, toys, quilts, and so forth, which have brought spectacular
profits to some collectors. These are the headline grabbers, the stories
that obscure the diligent work that in most cases precedes the profit
taking. If you are a prospective investor, you must, like the collector,
ask yourself some questions. How much money can you afford to set
aside for investment in antiques? Are you prepared to leave that money
alone for the long term? How much risk can you afford to take? Do you
have a sense of the market—what is a good price? What is scarce? What
is selling well?

If, after assessing your answers, you decide to go ahead, there are some basic guidelines you can follow.

1. Choose your area carefully. You may be drawn to certain fad items because they seem comparatively low in price right now. But it is far better, experts agree, to invest in items that have survived the test of time (preferably 100 years worth of time) and that are outstanding examples of a particular genre.
2. Learn all you can about your field.
3. Buy quality, but keep your purchase price as low as you possibly can.
4. Take the necessary precautions to protect your investment: burglar alarms, smoke detectors, insurance, and so forth. Keep careful records.
5. Think ahead about how and where and to whom you could sell the item.
6. Be prepared to hold on to your investment for the long term. Auctioneers and dealers say that it takes at least seven years for the wholesale prices at which you must sell to reach the retail level at which you most likely bought.

As it turns out, the advice for investors is basically the same as it is for collectors. After all, finding something of value that others have overlooked is one of the great pleasures of collecting.

The collector also has some other major advantages. Because he loves what he collects, he willingly spends time and energy learning about his field. Because he responds to an object with more than dollars and cents in mind, he is often more aware of an object's intrinsic worth. And finally, while he may also reap financial benefits in the long run, he is thoroughly enjoying himself in the meantime.

LEARNING ALL
YOU CAN

Every collector dreams of uncovering something rare or beautiful that no one else has recognized—and then acquiring it at a bargain price. Dreams do come true. You may be in the right place at the right time. But before you can cash in on your good luck, you have to know that what you want to buy is something worth having. More than thirty years ago Ruth Webb Lee, an authority on early American pressed glass, pointed out a simple fact: It takes knowledge to know when a bargain is really a bargain. And as prices rise relentlessly, knowledge becomes more and more essential for a collector.

The more you know the more your collection will benefit. Your knowledge will affect not only the price you are willing to pay for an item but your aesthetic judgments; not only the ultimate value of your collection but also your enjoyment of your hobby.

There are basically two ways to acquire the kind of knowledge we're talking about. The first is through your senses: your eyes, your ears, your hands. A certain sensitivity to objects (it can be instinctive or acquired) is essential for a collector. The second is through source materials: books, periodicals, courses, clubs, and so on.

Learning to look—really look—is a skill. As one dealer says, "It takes a lot of looking—and then you begin to see." Collectors who have spent some time at their hobby can walk through an antiques show, study each booth, and know in a glance if the object they are searching for is there. They can also tell if it's a fine specimen or a mediocre one.

Start to increase your powers of observation by examining an object slowly and carefully in good light. What size is it? What shape: round, oval, rectangular, irregular? What material is it made of? What kind of surface does it have: smooth or rough, shiny or matte? Are the edges sharp or rounded? Is there a design? A border? Carving? Decoration? Are there any markings? Are they impressed? Printed? Stenciled? Are there any signs of wear?

Collectors must learn to use their hands as well as their eyes in looking at an object. This is true for almost every specialty. If you are attuned to the feel of cut glass, you can run your hand over a candlestick and know from the sharpness of the edges if the piece is a fine example. Your hands will know even if the bell tone is missing (as it would be on an object shaped like a candlestick) or if the pattern does not match any you have seen in a book. If you study cast-iron mechanical banks, you will be able to run your hand over a bank, feel its smoothness or roughness, and know even before you trace the base plate whether the bank is genuine or a reproduction.

As your senses absorb information from an object's appearance, you will also be able to assess its age and its condition.

Dating any item is tricky; in the beginning you may want only a general idea—nineteenth century, say, or twentieth. Some definitions might be helpful. Antiques, as defined by the U.S. Tariff Act of 1930, are

> Works of art (except rugs and carpets made after the year 1700), collections in illustration of the progress of the arts, works in bronze, marble, terra cotta, parian, pottery, or porcelain, artistic antiquities, and objects of art of ornamental character or educational value which shall have been produced prior to the year 1830.

A strict interpretation of the law holds that only objects made before 1830 may be called antiques. But the regulation has been interpreted more loosely to include all objects that are 100 years old. Common usage has eroded the distinctions further, and nowadays some dealers and collectors will use the term *antique* to describe any item that has some historical or cultural significance.

The term *collectible,* a comparatively recent word, is defined in Webster's third edition, as "fit for a collection; suitable for being collected." That's not particularly enlightening. Common usage, luckily, is more helpful. *Collectible* has come to mean items that do not meet the objective criteria of *antique* but are still worth acquiring because of their beauty, scarcity, historical significance, oddity, or nostalgic connections. Within the scope of collectibles there is a wide divergence of standards, ranging from the discriminating collectors who will select objects that are not only rare but also extraordinary examples of craftsmanship, to the more casual who will collect whatever appeals to them, even if it was made yesterday in unlimited quantities.

Whatever you collect, antiques or collectibles, age is an important consideration. It determines where you find the object itself, where you find information about it, and perhaps how much you pay for it.

Condition is somewhat more difficult to pin down. Is an object in "fine" condition? Or "very fine" or "mint"? Only a trained eye can tell. You should see and touch the very best specimens you can find. After you know what an outstanding example looks like, then you can decide where to draw your own personal line of discrimination. Will you buy a Chinese export platter in the Fitzhugh pattern with age cracks? Will you buy a weathervane with a bullet hole? Will you pay the higher price for a mint postcard of the 1939 New York World's Fair?

Within each specialty there are different criteria for determining condition. Almost always, however, there is a relationship between condition and rarity or age. If an object is extremely rare even an advanced collector may buy one in less than mint condition. On the other hand, when an item is more readily available, collectors tend to trade-up until they have an almost perfect specimen.

You have, then, three areas—appearance, age, and condition—to consider as you examine an antique or a collectible. The more experienced you become, the more you will be able to rely on your senses. But you will probably still need more information. Fortunately, there is no lack of source materials to consult. In fact, the growing interest in antiques and collectibles has produced a wealth of books, magazines, newspapers, prices guides, museum exhibitions, courses, clubs.

Depending on your interest you will find certain sources more helpful than others. Some deal only with antiques; others with collectibles. Some will help you learn more about an item's background: when and where and how it was made; others will keep you in touch with the marketplace: who's selling, who's buying, and for how much. What follows is an examination of the various kinds of source materials. I have not tried to list every encyclopedia or every museum or every club. Rather, I have chosen to mention some outstanding examples and to offer collectors some criteria to use in making their selections.

SOURCE MATERIALS

There are many second-rate antiques and collectibles around; everyone admits that. We are not always so willing, however, to sift the second-rate authorities from the first-rate. Geoffrey A. Godden, who has published some fine source materials himself, writes "An enquiring or even a suspicious mind is one of the most valuable assets a collector can possess—no statement should be accepted as fact until it is rechecked."

Don't be too eager to accept the printed word. Items described as "unusual cheese baskets" may turn out to be ox muzzles. Such a casual slip may be humorous, but other misstatements can cost a collector money.

Caveat emptor ("Let the buyer beware") is a recognized warning when collectors enter the marketplace. The same warning, paraphrased, "Let the reader beware," should apply when a collector starts to look at source materials.

ENCYCLOPEDIAS, DICTIONARIES, SPECIALIZED BOOKS, DOCUMENTARY SOURCES

You will consult some books only once; you will look at others so often their bindings will soften and their corners curl. Some volumes will be helpful in the beginning and become less useful as you absorb all they can teach you. Some books you will want to buy and keep handy; others, the ones you will need only from time to time, you may prefer to borrow from a library.

If you're just beginning to collect, or moving into a new field, look first at some of the broad-ranging encyclopedias of antiques. These can be very helpful in pinning down basic facts. There are a great number of these encyclopedias or dictionaries on the market. Their approach and their quality vary. Compare several different volumes; you'll soon determine which ones are most helpful for you. Some authors choose to be as complete as possible and may sacrifice depth. Others go into greater detail but cover fewer areas. One encyclopedia, for example, gives a five-line summary of pressed glass while another devotes one-and-one-half columns to the same topic. Check out your field. A "complete" encyclopedia that does not include a listing for "stevengraphs" is not complete for you—if that's your interest.

When you reach the point that the information contained in such general reference books is no longer enough, you can select from a wide range of books that are devoted to each genre of antique or collectible. And within each category there are books that specialize in a certain country, a historical period, or a craftsman. If your specialty is pewter, silver, china, or glass, there are dozens of other books devoted solely to the identification marks used by manufacturers in various countries at various times.

And as interest in antiques and collectibles grows, publishers are finding ready markets for ever more specialized books. For many collectors the problem now is too much choice. How do you find books on your specialty? How do you decide which book (or books) to buy?

There are several ways to locate books on a particular subject. One place to begin is *Books in Print*. This reference work, which you'll find in bookstores and libraries, is published yearly and lists by title, author, and subject all the books currently in print in the United States. It will also give you the publisher and the price of hardbound and/or paperback editions. Another reference volume that you will find in many libraries, *Antiques and Collectibles: a Bibliography of Works in English*, lists books, pamphlets, and monographs published from the sixteenth century to 1976. Some of the more esoteric entries are available only in The British Museum or The Library of Congress. But you might find others in a local library or a second-hand bookstore.

Mail-order book outlets stock current books and some out-of-print or privately printed volumes. The firms that specialize in books about antiques and collectibles advertise heavily in antiques publications. Send for their free catalogues, but enclose a stamped self-addressed envelope. Below is a list of some of the largest firms that handle books on antiques and collectibles.

APOLLO BOOK
391 South Rd.
Poughkeepsie, N.Y. 12601
Art and antiques. Descriptions of books in catalogue.

BETHLEHEM BOOK CO.
249 East St.
Bethlehem, Conn. 06751
Many categories of antiques and collectibles. Descriptions.

CENTURY HOUSE
Watkins Glen, N.Y. 14891
Specialized books in limited editions. Descriptions.

COLLECTOR BOOKS
P.O. Box 3009
Paducah, Ky. 42001
Many categories. Some brief descriptions.

EDMONDS BOOKS SALES
P.O. Box 143
Ledbetter, Ky. 42058
Many categories. Brief coded descriptions.

GAZETTE BOOKS
Box 1011
Kermit, Tex. 79745
Many categories. No descriptions.

HOTCHKISS HOUSE
18 Hearthstone Rd.
Pittsford, N.Y. 14534
Many categories. Descriptions.

HOUSE OF COLLECTIBLES
773 Kirkman Road N. 120
Orlando, Fla. 32811
Mostly price guides, coins, and stamps.

L-W BOOK SALES
Box 69
Gas City, Ind. 46933
Many categories. No descriptions.

THE REFERENCE RACK, INC.
Box 445 C
Orefield, Pa. 18069
Many categories. No descriptions.

WALLACE-HOMESTEAD BOOK CO.
1912 Grand Ave.
Des Moines, Iowa 50305
Many categories. Descriptions.

The more books you look at the more obvious certain criteria will become to you. Although it's true you cannot tell a book by its cover, you can get some clues from the title and contents pages. First of all, will the book tell you what you want to know? Check the chapter headings. How is the book organized? Can you find what you want easily? Do you need illustrations? If so, are they there? How many? Is there an index? A bibliography? Is the information up-to-date? Check the copyright date. That will tell you when the book was published. Some books like Wallace Nutting's *Furniture Treasury* were published in the 1920s or 1930s, but still remain classic source materials and are reprinted over and over. Other books suffer because the most recent information available on a particular field is not included. One good test is to look up a fact you already know. Is the information there? Is it correct? Is it complete?

For the collector who wants to delve even further into the background of an object, there are several primary sources to be explored.

Trademark and patent papers. If the object was patented—and it may surprise you to learn how many kinds of things are protected by a patent—then it is possible to get a copy of the original patent papers. Information on them includes the name of the inventor and the name of the manufacturer plus the date, a description, and often a drawing of the object as the inventor saw it.

When you have the patent number, you can request a copy of the papers directly from the Patent Office in Washington, D.C. If you know the year the patent was granted and the type of object or the name of the inventor, you can research the number in the *Official Gazette of the U.S. Patent Office,* which is available in many libraries. If you do not have that information, you'll probably need help from one of the regional depositories for government information.

A manufacturer who wanted to protect his name or symbol registered his *trademark* with the Patent Office. *The Trademark Register of the United States* publishes all current trademarks registered and renewed since 1818. It gives you the date and the number; you follow up in the *Official Gazette.* (Trademarks and patents are now separated in the gazette; they were combined in the early editions.)

Many items were protected by two kinds of patents plus a trademark. A nineteenth-century manufacturer of spoons, for example, would first protect his method of making spoons with a patent; perhaps protect the appearance of a particular piece with a design patent; and the name and symbol of his company with a trademark. Today's collector who specializes in commemorative spoons might therefore learn a great deal about witch spoons or George and Martha Washington spoons by examining patent and trademark papers.

Advertising paper. When many of today's collectibles first came on the market, manufacturers, jobbers, and mail-order houses such as Sears, Roebuck and Montgomery Ward all produced catalogues, often with quite lavish illustrations. These volumes are now valuable sources of information for identifying unusual items, reaffirming known items, checking original wholesale and retail prices, and in general getting a feel for the period. Catalogues have become collectors' items in themselves. Less "collectible" but still informative are the many reprints of old catalogues that are on the market today.

Contemporary periodicals. A magazine like *Godey's Lady's Book* can provide insights into the background of a particular antique or collectible. So can diaries, estate inventory lists, trade directories, and catalogues from early museum exhibitions. Keep your eye open for such material wherever you go.

PERIODICALS

Antiques newspapers and magazines not only provide essential background information on a variety of subjects, they also keep their readers up-to-date on the market. They spot trends. They put dealers in touch with collectors, collectors in touch with dealers, collectors in touch with other collectors. Some of the best of the so-called trade publications have been in business for many years; they're dependable and speak with authority. But some promising newcomers on the scene also deserve attention.

These days you'll find many of the periodicals available at newsstands or in libraries. Most of those that are not widely distributed will send a sample copy on request. Look it over carefully. Are you primarily interested in developments in the marketplace? Then one of the publications filled with column after column of advertising will be useful. If, on the other hand, you're looking for background information, you'll only be frustrated by those same columns.

Some magazines excel in scholarly research; others do a fine job of independent news reporting; still others are filled with press releases masquerading as informative articles. Decide what you want from a publication and then choose the one you think does it best. You may discover, as many collectors do, that you need a combination of periodicals to fulfill different needs.

Here are some other things you might want to think about as you look over a periodical.

1. *How frequently is it published?* Some newspapers are published weekly; others monthly. Some magazines appear bimonthly or even quarterly. Does it matter to you that you have last-minute news of auctions and shows?

2. *Does it cover your specialty on a regular basis?* There's no sense in sub-

scribing to a publication that specializes in the European market when you collect Indian artifacts.

3. *Is there a geographic slant to the coverage,* either in reporting or in advertising? Some publications attract advertising mainly from New England; others from the Middle Atlantic states; still others from the Midwest, South, or West.

4. Take a look at the regular features in the publication. *Is there a calendar of shows, auctions, flea markets?* Most publications offer something along that line. *Is there a Question and Answer column? Are there letters from readers?* These features can often be a good source of extra information. *Is there an index to advertisers?* It's helpful if you want to find a particular dealer's ad quickly.

The following list of periodicals includes newspapers, magazines, and newsletters that will be of interest to a broad range of collectors. The capsule descriptions will give you frequency of publication, subscription information, editorial focus, specialties, and geographic emphasis, if any. (The letter *M* at the beginning of the review indicates the publication is primarily for information about the marketplace. The letter *B* indicates it is primarily helpful in providing background information.)

American Collector
Drawer C
Kermit, Tex. 79745
MONTHLY. SUBSCRIPTION: $20.00 a year; includes membership in the American Collector Club.
(B) *Tabloid newspaper with both articles and regular columns on toys, dolls, pottery, bottles, and other collectibles. Offerings for limited editions. Show calendar; Q and A column. Minimal display advertising; more classified advertising. Membership in club entitles you to bartering privileges.*

Americana
Americana Magazine Inc.
475 Park Ave. South
New York, N.Y. 10016
BIMONTHLY. SUBSCRIPTION: $11.90 a year.
(B) *A practical magazine that is not just for collectors. Includes articles on places to go and things to do or make as well as on American antiques or collectibles. Some classified advertising.*

Antique Monthly
Boone Inc.
P.O. Drawer 2
Tuscaloosa, Ala. 35402
MONTHLY. SUBSCRIPTION: $14.00 a year.

(M) *A newspaper for collectors of fine European and American furniture, paintings, and decorative arts. Some articles. Some color illustrations. Book reviews; Q and A columns on furniture and on miscellaneous items. Limited paid directory of services, shops, and museums. Heavy dealer advertising.*

The Antique Trader Weekly
Babka Publishing Co. Inc.
Box 1050
Dubuque, Iowa 52001
WEEKLY. SUBSCRIPTION: $19.00 a year.

(M) *A tabloid newspaper. Widely read for its advertising. Forty categories of ads, including buttons, dolls, guns, and bottles. Good coverage of plate and Hummel specialties. Calendar by region. Lengthy dealer listings for mail-order collectors. Auction and show advertising has good Midwest coverage.*

Antiques and the Arts Weekly
The Newtown Bee
Newtown, Conn. 06470
WEEKLY. SUBSCRIPTION: $15.00 a year.

(M) *Newspaper. Focus on antiques rather than collectibles; on the American market rather than the European. Short news articles; auction reports with prices and pictures. Every February publishes yearly schedule of shows and flea markets, predominantly in Northeast and Midatlantic states. Heavy dealer advertising. Heavy auction advertising. Heavy show advertising, emphasizing the East and Northeast.*

The Antiques Journal
Babka Publishing Co. Inc.
Box 1046
Dubuque, Iowa 52001
MONTHLY. SUBSCRIPTION: $11.00 a year.

(B) *Magazine. Several long articles each month with a wide range of subjects, for example, quilts and sleigh bells. Plus current prices for selected antiques. Book reviews, Q and A column. Listing of shows. Some dealer advertising; classified.*

Antiques Observer
Suite 8A
3545 Chain Bridge Rd.
Fairfax, Va. 22030

MONTHLY. SUBSCRIPTION: $8.00 a year.

(M) *Tabloid newspaper. Covers antiques and collectibles. Strong regional—Virginia/Maryland—slant. Show calendar. Heavy dealer advertising.*

Antiques USA
P.O. Box 974
Kermit, Tex. 79745
MONTHLY. SUBSCRIPTION: $25.00 a year.

(M) *Combines* ANTIQUE PRICE REPORT *with* ANTIQUING IN TEXAS. *Published in 5 regional editions. Articles are both national and regional in scope; so is advertising. Price lists deemphasized. Travel, decorating. Dealer directory.*

Antiques World
Antiques News Associates
122 East 42nd St.
New York, N.Y. 10168
MONTHLY except June, July, and August (combined issue). SUBSCRIPTION: $18.00 a year.

(B) *A new magazine covering quality American and European antiques. Market news, behind-the-scenes reports on auctions, appraisals. Decorating with antiques. Book reviews. Heavy dealer advertising.*

Art and Antiques
Billboard Publications
1515 Broadway
New York, N.Y. 10036
BIMONTHLY. SUBSCRIPTION: $21.00 a year.

(B) *Another newcomer on the scene; magazine format. In-depth feature articles on quality furniture, paintings, posters, architecture. Full color. Regular columns on restoration, preservation, the marketplace, insurance, and security. Cumulative 6-month index. Dealer advertising.*

Art and Auction
The Auction Guild
250 West 57th St.
New York, N.Y. 10019
TEN TIMES A YEAR. SUBSCRIPTION: $25 a year.

(M) *A new magazine that reports news of the auction world. Previews of upcoming sales; reviews of past sales. Good coverage of New York galleries as well as others throughout United States and in Europe. Calendar by type of sale and date. Predominantly auction advertising.*

Canadian Antiques and Art Review
P.O. Box 3664
Halifax South
Nova Scotia, B3J 3K6
TEN TIMES A YEAR. SUBSCRIPTION: $24.00 a year outside Canada; $21.00 in Canada.
(B) *Another new magazine; devoted to Canadian antiques market. News; background; practical advice. Information on shows and auctions. Book reviews. Calendar. Some dealer advertising.*

Collector Editions Quarterly
Acquire Publishing Co. Inc.
170 Fifth Ave.
New York, N.Y. 10010
FIVE TIMES A YEAR. SUBSCRIPTION: $8.50 a year.
(M, B) *Formerly ACQUIRE magazine, covers primarily limited-edition markets, but also touches on other collectibles. Regular auction notes plus columns on Hummels, porcelain, coins, plates. Advertising from dealers and distributors of limited editions.*

Collectors News
Box 156
Grundy Center, Iowa 50638
MONTHLY. SUBSCRIPTION: $10.00 a year.
(M) *Tabloid newspaper; heavy advertising. More than 60 categories of ads, such as weapons, Orientalia, insulators. Articles are organized to appear near ads on the same subject. Some columns, including the Kovels' Q and A. Also a Hummel Q and A and a postcard Q and A. Calendar has good Midwest coverage. Very heavy limited-editions advertising. Auction advertising.*

Early American Life
Early American Society
P.O. Box 1607
Marion, Ohio 43302
BIMONTHLY. MEMBERSHIP: $12.00 a year (includes subscription).
(B) *Magazine devoted to full range of early American interests: food, flowers, and customs, as well as houses and antiques. Travel coverage. Calendar of events. Q and A column. Book reviews. Classified advertising; readers' exchange column to help you locate hard-to-find items.*

Flea Market U.S.A.
Rte. 1, Box 470
Cantonment, Fla. 32533
QUARTERLY. SUBSCRIPTION: $12.00 yearly plus $1.00 postage; single copy $3 plus $1 postage.

(M) *A directory of flea markets, swap meets, trade days. Includes coast-to-coast listings.*

The Gray Letter
P.O. Drawer 2
Tuscaloosa, Ala. 35402
WEEKLY. SUBSCRIPTION: $75.00 a year.
(M) *A four-page newsletter that covers the same general areas as* ANTIQUE MONTHLY: *American and European painting, furniture, and decorative arts. Auction reports with prices achieved. Other information and "inside" news are primarily of interest to dealers, museum curators, and some advanced collectors.*

Hobbies
1006 South Michigan Ave.
Chicago, Ill. 60605
MONTHLY. SUBSCRIPTION: $12.00 a year.
(M, B) *Magazine; a traditional source of information for collectors. Columns on dolls, old glass and china, clocks, buttons, mechanical banks, firearms, coins, Indian relics. Advertising keyed to similar areas. Many display ads; many dealer listings for orders by mail. Show listings have good Midwest coverage.*

Joel Sater's Antiques and Auction News
Box B
Marietta, Pa. 17547
BIWEEKLY. SUBSCRIPTION: $6.00 a year; free through dealers or at auction houses.
(M) *Tabloid; brief news items on collectors and collectibles, museums, exhibitions, and auctions. Calendar. Heavy show, auction, and flea market advertising, primarily in Midatlantic states. Classified advertising.*

Kovels on Antiques and Collectables
P.O. Box 22200
Beachwood, Ohio 44122
MONTHLY. Subscription: $25.00 a year.
(M, B) *12-page newsletter, published by two well-known figures in the antiques world. Coverage is broad but brief. Auction reports with prices and some illustrations; dictionary of marks; news on reproductions, lectures, exhibitions. Mini book reviews. Q and A column.*

The Magazine *Antiques*
Straight Enterprises
551 Fifth Ave.
New York, N.Y. 10017
MONTHLY. SUBSCRIPTION: $38.00 a year.

(M, B) *The giant in the field. An impressive, beautifully illustrated magazine written for the collector of quality European and American antiques. Articles are scholarly. Book reviews. Calendar. Lavish dealer advertising with full-color illustrations. Variety of smaller paid listings: historic homes, dealers, shows, and sales.*

Maine Antique Digest
Box 358
Waldoboro, Me. 04572
MONTHLY. SUBSCRIPTION: $23.00 a year.

(M, B) *Newspaper; considered essential for collectors of American antiques. Covers painting, furniture, folk art, toys, firearms. Emphasis on news rather than background, although both are covered. Excellent coverage of auctions and shows. Informative reader's forum. Calendar. Very heavy dealer advertising. Advertising for shows and auctions has New England emphasis.*

Ohio Antique Review
P.O. Box 538
Worthington, Ohio 43085
MONTHLY EXCEPT JANUARY. SUBSCRIPTION: $15.00 a year.

(M) *Tabloid newspaper focusing on American antiques. Format similar to* MAINE ANTIQUE DIGEST. *Strong midwestern regional slant. Good coverage, including photographs, of shows and auctions. Heavy dealer advertising.*

Sotheby Parke Bernet Newsletter
980 Madison Ave.
New York, N.Y. 10021
TEN TIMES A YEAR. SUBSCRIPTION: $3.00.

(M) *A 16-page newsletter. Of interest primarily to those who follow the international auction market. Includes full schedule of upcoming SPB auctions with black-and-white illustrations of highlighted items. Details on absentee bidding included. Some reports on prices achieved at past SPB sales. An occasional article on appraisals or news of a seminar.*

Spinning Wheel
Everybody's Press Inc.
Hanover, Pa. 17331
BIMONTHLY. SUBSCRIPTION: $12.00 a year.

(B) *Magazine; published by American Antique and Crafts Society. Covers a wide range of antiques and collectibles. Strong on dolls, ceramics, glass, kitchen items, metals. Q and A column. Listing of shows and shops has coast-to-coast coverage. Auction previews; some past prices also included. Classified advertising.*

In addition to these general periodicals, there are many other publications that are aimed at narrower segments of the collecting public. These magazines and newspapers often take on a quite different tone. They assume a closer relationship with their readers. The editors write chatty columns about their travels and their families; they pass along personal news about collectors and dealers. These publications, whether they are devoted to toys, bottles, or plates, are usually a good mixture of advertising and articles. The material included in the columns and articles presumes some knowledge on the part of the reader. Lists of reproductions, for example, may be written in a kind of shorthand. Occasionally a key letter or number will refer readers to standard reference books in the field.

A good source for information about the specialty publications is the advertising columns of the more general newspapers and magazines. Or you may happen on a copy at a show or in a dealer's shop. Because these publications usually operate on a very limited budget, they often request that you pay for a sample issue.

PRICE GUIDES

In a constantly changing market it is difficult to find any price that stays the same long enough to gather it into a guide. It's also difficult to find agreement among dealers and collectors about which prices should be included. Is a Zanesville bottle worth the $180 it brought at an auction in Delaware or the $260 a dealer asked at a show in Chicago?

Still, price guides are an essential source of information for any collector. As long as you remember that there can be no "official" price on any antique or collectible, the guides can help you form an educated guess about what you may have to pay for a particular item. You can also use the information to arrive at an informal appraisal of your collection and for guidance when you want to sell an item.

Beyond these basic uses many of the guides also function as mini-encyclopedias, giving a short informative paragraph before each category of prices. In Kovels', for example, you could find out that Gaudy Dutch pottery is white earthenware with red, blue, green, yellow, and black decoration; that it was made in England for export to America from around 1810 to 1820. Some of the guides take note of items that have been reproduced.

If over the years you build a library of price guides, you'll find them to be an interesting source of information on market trends. You can get a good idea of what kinds of items are "hot" by comparing prices in different years. While single prices within a category may be out of line, an entire category can usually be counted on to spell out a trend. The authors of the guides will often point out such trends in a preface.

In addition to the general guides listed below, there are many many others that specialize in specific areas such as dolls, comic books, collector plates, bottles, cut glass, prints. Whenever you consult a price guide, check the date of publication. Prices may be out-of-date. And check the method the editors used to compile the prices. It will help you to assess the information you find inside if you know whether the guide was compiled from figures supplied solely by auction houses, solely by dealers, or a combination of both.

The Antique Trader Price Guide to Antiques and Collectors' Items. Babka Publishing Co., Inc., Dubuque, Iowa 52001. Quarterly. Subscription: $7.00 a year; single copy $2.00. Alphabetical by category; some descriptive paragraphs. Illustrations. Usually features one category of antique or collectible: baskets or kitchenware. Article plus extensive price coverage of that category.

Flea Market Trader III. Steve Quertermous, Collector Books, Paducah, Ky. 42001. $7.95. Revised 1980 edition. Alphabetical by category. No museum-quality antiques. Cross section of flea market items from advertising buttons to fruit jars to sheet music. Illustrations. Informative paragraphs.

The Kovels' Complete Antiques Price List. Thirteenth edition. Ralph and Terry Kovel, Crown Publishers, New York, N.Y. 10016. $9.95. Alphabeti-cal by category; paragraphs before each category describe items and note reproductions. Illustrations.

Lyle Official Antiques Review. Lyle Publications, Glenmayne, Galashiels, Scotland. $14.95. Revised yearly. Alphabetical by category; every item sketched. Brief descriptions. Primarily English auction prices on furniture and decorative arts. Index.

Pictorial Price Guide to American Antiques. Dorothy Hammond, E.P. Dutton, New York, N.Y. 10016. $9.95. Fourth edition in 1981. Alphabetical by category. Every item photographed. Prices keyed to dealer (D) or auction (A) with state and year. Condition of item often included.

Price Guide to Antiques and Pattern Glass. Seventh Edition. Edited by Robert W. Miller. Wallace-Homestead Book Co., Des Moines, Iowa 50305. $10.95. Revised yearly. Alphabetical by category. Introductory paragraphs describe entries. Photographs.

Warmans' Antiques and Their Prices. P. S. Warman, E. G. Warman Publications, Inc., Uniontown, Pa. 15401.

$10.95. Warman published its first guide in 1949. *15th Antiques* appeared in 1980. Alphabetical by category. Paragraph before each category provides basic information. Reproduced items marked with asterisk. Illustrations; index.

AUCTION CATALOGUES

Most of the large auction houses publish catalogues for their important sales. So do a number of smaller, more specialized auction galleries. The catalogues can be simple or lavish. And you may have to work your way through some enthusiastic verbiage. Almost everything is "rare," "fine," "important," or "highly important."

But you can learn a great deal from auction catalogues—about the background of certain objects as well as about their market value. At the very least you will find out what's currently available in your field. (Important information about conditions of sale, reserves, and credit lines also appears in most catalogues. Because these aspects involve actual bidding, they are covered in "How—and Where—to Buy," p. 39ff.)

The better catalogues have clear photographs; they provide a brief description of each item, including its period, identifying marks, and condition. Learn to read the descriptions carefully. Notice what has been left out as well as what's been said. Is there a date? A manufacturer? Is the settee Duncan Phyfe or simply Phyfe-style?

Many auction houses include in their catalogues presale estimates: their educated guess about what each item will bring at auction. The prices are usually given in a range ($250–$400). These figures represent the opinions of the auctioneer's staff—a compilation of their knowledge, their experience, their intuition. They can be wrong, of course, for the antiques market is a volatile one. More often than not the estimates come close to the final prices realized.

If you attend the sale, you will find out for yourself. If you do not, some auction houses will provide postsale price lists for a small fee (usually $1.00 or $2.00). A comparison between the presale estimates and postsale prices can yield some interesting information. Whereas the estimates represent educated guesses from people knowledgeable in the field, the prices report what was actually paid for the item on a particular day in a particular city or town. (There is one exception. Auction houses differ in their policies of reporting buy-ins, that is, items returned to the consignor. Some do not include these in postsale lists, others do.)

The postsale figures, therefore, may reflect something as fleeting as the weather. They may also reflect the audience's overall mood of delight or disenchantment. They may reflect a bidding war between two people—each enamored of a figurine and each determined to have it. In any case, when you have both presale estimates and final prices, you know what the experts think the item is worth and you also know what someone actually paid for it.

It is worth building up your own collection of auction catalogues. Some houses offer subscriptions to all their catalogues. These are expensive and of value primarily to dealers. You can also buy a subscription to catalogues in your specialty, for example, Oriental rugs. Or you can buy only individual catalogues as they appeal to you.

Two of the largest international auction houses, Sotheby Parke Bernet and Christie's (both have salesrooms in New York and Europe), also publish luxurious annual volumes (see bibliography) that give highlights of their sales during the previous year. The books are designed to be reference works. Both cover a full range of categories, are lavishly illustrated, and include sale price and date. Both have authoritative articles on a variety of subjects. And both are expensive.

MUSEUMS

Since the seventeenth century museums have played an important role in the lives of collectors. The reverse is also true, of course. Most of the great museums, and the smaller ones, too, owe their existence to collectors who wanted not only to keep their treasures together but also share them with the public. Today's collectors turn to museums for guidance and information; the museums provide help in a variety of ways.

There are, first of all, the permanent collections, the objects on display or in storage that are routinely available for study. Large city museums, where antiques are often collected in separate galleries or wings; small local museums, specializing in one area or another; and historical restorations all function as memory banks. There you can see fine examples of objects in your field. There you can develop your eye and refine your judgment.

In addition to making their permanent collections available to collectors, museums also put on special exhibitions. Occasionally such an exhibition captures the public's enthusiasm to such an extent that a whole new field of collecting opens up. Objects that were out of favor are once again smiled upon; the demand for them increases, and, inevitably, prices soar. That happened after the 1970 exhibition "Nineteenth-Century America" at The Metropolitan Museum of Art in New York. The event threw a spotlight on American Victorian furniture, and, with the increase in demand that ensued, prices on prime examples more than doubled. The catalogue for that exhibition was not popular at the time but, ironically, it has since become an important source book for dealers and collectors specializing in Victorian design.

Not all special exhibitions have such dramatic results. More frequently museums respond to the public's taste rather than try to set trends or blaze new trails. Any exhibit, no matter how small, can be helpful if it teaches you something about your field.

A survey of museums across the country shows that attendance figures are up for both the permanent collections and the special exhibitions. It also shows that the majority of institutions, both public and private, are trying to provide information for collectors in a variety of other ways.

Publications. Some institutions, like Colonial Williamsburg in Virginia, publish extensive lists of books, films, and slides. Others maintain excellent libraries. The Corning Museum of Glass in New York, for example, has 25,000 volumes plus trade catalogues, prints, and films available for research. Many museums publish newsletters, brochures, and handbooks. The Newark Museum devotes each issue of its quarterly publication to a specific subject, such as Chinese ceramics or dollhouses. The Cincinnati Art Museum published *Collector's Handbook* (see bibliography), which is filled with practical information any collector can use.

Educational programs: forums, seminars, courses, lectures and tours. Some of the most famous forums have been in existence for many years. Colonial Williamsburg has conducted its three-day winter forum for more than thirty years. The New York State Historical Association in Cooperstown has been running its week-long summer seminars on American culture for about the same length of time. The Henry Ford Museum in Dearborn, Michigan, has offered its "Midwest Antiques Forum" every fall for more than twenty years. In Massachusetts Old Sturbridge Village offers its traditional "Antiques Collectors' Weekend" every fall and Historic Deerfield presents several forums on a variety of subjects, such as ceramics, glass, or clocks, in both the spring and the fall.

Other museums, which do not perhaps have the facilities to provide food and lodging, offer collectors different kinds of educational experiences: one-day seminars, evening lectures, luncheon talks. All of the programs seem to be successful. One curator reported that when they first scheduled a one-day seminar, they worried about filling the 400-seat auditorium. Now, he says, they worry about oversubscription months before a seminar even takes place.

Often these programs are presented in conjunction with a local university or adult-education school, and in many cases the lecturers are drawn from larger museums in the area.

Curators themselves are in demand as speakers at events outside the museum. They teach college-level courses as well as adult-education classes. They are invited to garden clubs and historical societies. Museum personnel are also the drawing card for seminars and forums that are sponsored by universities or independent organizations.

Curators also travel. Museums sponsor tours to other museums, to private collections, to antiques shows, to foreign countries. The attraction of these tours is not only the destination and the pleasure of sharing the events with people of similar interests but also the presence of the curator. If a curator goes, one museum spokeswoman pointed out bluntly, the trip sells out faster.

Identification days. These events are a fairly recent development and, museums report, very popular. The public is invited to bring items to the museum for inspection and evaluation. The method of operation varies. In some cases the museum's own curators examine the items, either on a regular once-a-month schedule or on an informal "bring it in" basis. Curators carefully avoid giving any monetary value, such as a probable selling price.

Other museums ask experts from well-known auction houses to give their opinions. Many institutions have found that it is impractical to hold "discovery days" too often, and so these events may be scheduled on an annual or biannual basis.

Responding to inquiries. Almost all museums report a great increase in the number of inquiries they receive from collectors. One curator welcomes the added interest; another suspects that some collectors are taking the easy way out, calling the experts for an answer they could find themselves with a little effort. In any case telephone calls and letters do receive attention from the museums' staffs, if they are able to handle the volume.

But there is a limit to what they will do. Museums will not, for instance, give appraisals. They prefer not to identify anything without seeing it in person or in a photograph. They may supply the name of a restorer, weaver, or other craftsman, but they will not guarantee the work. Do not ask them to give an opinion about a certain dealer; suggest a "fair price" to pay for an item; select colors for a wall; or offer auction advice. They will, in most cases, try to be as helpful as they can, particularly for a collector they believe is truly interested in an object, not just in its marketability.

In addition to local newspapers and travel guides there are two good sources for information about museums and their exhibits. *The Official Museum Directory,* published by The American Association of Museums and available in most libraries, lists all institutions alphabetically by state, then by city or town. There is an index by category: antiques, history, folk art, railroad, and so forth. *Treasures of America,* published by the Reader's Digest (see bibliography), uses a somewhat confusing geographic breakdown, but is otherwise very helpful in identifying and locating museums that may be of interest to collectors.

PEOPLE: DEALERS, OTHER COLLECTORS, AND CLUBS

Museums, despite their numerous treasures, are not the only, or necessarily the best, source of information for collectors. There are many collectors whose specialties are not yet housed in museums—and perhaps they never will be. There are also many collectors who find the hands-off policy of museums too inhibiting. As one of these collectors puts it, "I prefer to be where I can not only see it but smell it and feel it." These collectors believe that the best way to learn is from other people.

Russell Lynes, in his book *The Tastemakers,* suggests that in the life of every collector there is someone, a "tastemaker"—dealer, decorator, artist, expert of some kind—who guides him through the market. Many collectors readily agree this is true; the relationship between a knowledgeable dealer and an enthusiastic collector is of benefit to both. You learn about the background of your specialty as well as about the marketplace from an interested dealer. You must be willing to pay for this expertise, for the prices of a reputable dealer will reflect his knowledge and experience. On the other side of the coin, dealers willingly share their knowledge, experience, and taste with collectors who are interested in similar objects. In return they can count on steady customers.

Beginning collectors often find shows and flea markets particularly informative, not only because they provide an opportunity to see many objects at one time but also because a show gives them an opportunity to meet and evaluate different dealers. It is often easier in such a setting to get a sense of whether you and a particular dealer have something in common. You can not only see what he sells—and at what price—but you can also listen in on conversations that go on around you. Ask questions yourself. Don't be too hasty. Not all dealers are knowledgeable. Many have only been in the business for a few years; you may find you know more than they do. Be skeptical until you're sure you've found someone who *really* knows.

An excellent source of information is another collector. It may turn out that someone you see at an auction every Wednesday night is also a collector of Currier & Ives lithographs. You may be invited to see his collection. You may have something to learn from each other. Such chance encounters are rewarding and stimulating.

There are also many clubs and organizations around the country that help collectors keep in touch with other collectors of the same items. These organizations range from the giant, well-established National Association of Watch and Clock Collectors, Inc., with 30,000 members and a thirty-eight-year history, to the smaller and more recent Pen Fancier's Club or Cookie Cutter Collector's Club.

Some clubs set up rather rigid membership guidelines. The Mechanical Bank Collectors Club requires that prospective members own at least five mechanical banks. The Antique Toy Collectors of America limits the number of new members to twelve a year—and has a waiting list. Some require sponsorship by a member and approval by a committee or a board of directors. Others ask only that you send in an application and pay your dues. Whatever the requirements, once you are a member, you are eligible to participate in all activities and receive a copy of all publications.

Most of the clubs publish some kind of newsletter. At the very least the newsletters provide a schedule of upcoming events and news about members, but often they do a great deal more. Members contribute articles on a particular item they've recently uncovered; editors provide listings of reproductions and fakes; report on recent purchases and "finds." Many newsletters publish trading columns or allow members to list their "wants" free of charge. Membership rosters are controversial. Some clubs no longer allow them; others do but permit members to withhold their names if they wish. Occasionally clubs also publish glossy bulletins or quarterly magazines that include scholarly articles on their specialty.

The major event of the year for most club members is the convention. This is not only a social occasion and a chance to visit a place that may have special significance for club members. It is also an opportunity to improve your collection. Despite the careful planning and strict procedures set up by various clubs, conventions (or *canventions* as the Tin Container Collectors Association calls them) tend to be freewheeling occasions. The scheduled events usually include informal talks, slide show presentations, and exhibits. But the highlight of the weekend is the auction, show, sale, or swap meet—whatever arrangement works best for the membership. In addition to this organized way of buying and selling items, members spend their off-hours, usually the early morning hours, visiting other members' rooms, buying, selling, and trading some more.

Many of the clubs find other ways to help members with their collections. Deltiologists (those who collect postcards) sponsor frequent mail auctions; other clubs sponsor regional swap meets or sales. Some organizations are able to offer their members research assistance. The National Association of Watch and Clock Collectors, Inc., has a museum, a library, and its headquarters in Columbia, Pennsylvania. The Heisey Collectors of America established their own museum in Newark, Ohio. This combination of providing market outlets as well as background research is the reason many collectors find their clubs such a valuable resource.

One somewhat different organization, Questers, includes among its members many different kinds of collectors. While its primary purpose is to help members learn about the background of various historical artifacts, the organization, on both national and local levels, also provides support for a variety of historic landmarks. Questers maintains a headquarters and library at 210 South Quince St., Philadelphia, Pennsylvania 19107.

It is not always so easy to find the addresses of other collectors' clubs.

The *Encyclopedia of Associations,* published yearly by Gale Publications and available in most public libraries, lists quite a few clubs, but by no means all of them. In addition not all libraries can afford to buy this volume yearly and outdated volumes often have outdated addresses. *The New Collector's Directory* (see bibliography) also lists many organizations.

MISCELLANEOUS SOURCES

It may seem that once you've read the books, magazines, newspapers, and newsletters in your field, visited museums, restorations, and historic sites, talked to dealers and other collectors, you've exhausted all the avenues for learning. And you will certainly have covered the main ones. But the tremendous interest in antiques and collectibles has opened up a few other possibilities. Although you may not learn a great deal from these sources, there is always the random piece of information that, like a dusty volume at the bottom of the carton, may prove valuable.

1. *Articles in magazines. Vogue, Woman's Day, Good Housekeeping, House Beautiful, New York, Changing Times,* and *Business Week* have all published articles recently on buying and selling antiques. These articles are usually more general than those you'll find in trade publications but you may find their broad overview gives you new insights into the market. Check the *Reader's Guide to Periodical Literature* under "antiques" or "collecting" for specific articles.

2. *Newspaper columns.* Several papers publish excellent columns on antiques. *The New York Times* covers the auction scene on Friday and the more general world of antiques and collectibles on Sunday.

Many local newspapers publish syndicated Question and Answer columns on antiques. Your chances of finding information on your specialty are slim. But you can submit questions to these columnists. Some will answer your questions personally if you enclose a stamped self-addressed envelope. Others will publish your question with an answer if they believe the subject is of interest to enough of their readers.

Whenever you submit a question to a Q and A column, be as explicit as you can. The more you tell them about the item, the more they will be able to tell you. Send a clear photograph if you have one, or make a sketch. Describe the item as fully as you can; give its size, color, condition, and so forth. If there is an identification mark not visible in the photograph or sketch, copy it down. If the mark is impressed and too faint to read, make a rubbing (place a thin piece of paper over the mark, then rub back and forth with a very soft pencil until you see the impression of the mark on the paper). Remember that Q and A columns are not appraisal services, although some columns will give broad evaluations such as "in the low hundreds."

3. *Television.* An unusual source of information that has only recently become available to many collectors is the televised charity auction. The most famous auction is for the benefit of WNET/Channel 13 in New York, where the annual art and antiques auction not only raises more than a million dollars but teaches millions of viewers things they never knew about antiques. In your own home, at your leisure, you can listen to the opinions of the authorities, watch the bidding—and learn.

MISTAKES

There will come a time sooner or later, no matter how much you learn, when you will be fooled. You will buy an "original" and discover it is a reproduction. You will buy a "perfect" object and find it has been repaired.

Take heart; you certainly are not alone. Almost every collector has made mistakes. Henry Francis du Pont, who founded the great Winterthur Museum near Wilmington, Delaware, would often say to someone whose collection he had just seen: "You've shown me your treasures. Now show me your fakes." For years curators at the Corning Museum of Glass believed they had a sixteenth-century Venetian goblet on display. They have recently discovered that the goblet is a fake: it was made not in the sixteenth century but in the nineteenth.

Painstaking forgeries, perfect to almost the last detail, are most likely to occur in high-priced specialties. It takes time and money to produce such a good copy. For the average buyer the threat is more likely to come from ordinary reproductions masquerading as originals.

The best way to protect yourself is to learn about reproductions as well as original pieces. Remember that a reproduction is not a threat until it pretends to be something it is not. Then it becomes a "fake." There are many honest reproductions. Museums produce some high-quality examples in both furniture and the decorative arts. Other reproductions are sold in gift shops and through mail-order catalogues. The problem arises when someone decides to represent these honest items as genuine antiques. Often all you'll need to do to detect the fake is place the suspicious item next to an authentic piece. If you're interested in Depression glass, for example, put a plate in the original Cherry Blossom pattern next to one of the reproductions made in the 1970s. You will be able to tell immediately which plate is the original. (In this instance the pattern on the reproduction does not extend to the rim.) Modern Toby jugs, steins, and Staffordshire figurines also come off poorly when compared to an original. The workmanship is just not fine enough.

Another troublesome area for collectors is the rebuilt piece, one assembled from parts of different objects. *Marriages,* as they're called, occur in many specialties. In furniture a tabletop may not belong with the legs. In candlesticks the upright may be joined to an improper base. In toys, wheels and other parts as often interchanged. A horse-drawn toy up for bidding at a recent auction was made up of pieces from three different manufacturers. The auctioneer's comment: "They all got together on this," provided a light moment—and made the marriage clear.

If you like dolls, you may find a lovely creature with an appropriate marking at the base of the back of the neck. And you may assume that arms, legs, and torso are of the same maker and period. You would have to know about the style and the technique of that particular manufacturer to recognize that although the creature may be lovely, she is also "married."

To steer clear of marriages, look for clues in design and construction. Know what Queen Anne legs should look like; how a doll's arms should be attached; how the lid on a blanket chest should open. Even in the field of ceramics, where marriages are not so likely, you should know the characteristics of earthenware, stoneware, and porcelain. You should be able to identify the kind of glaze and method of decoration that was used in the type of piece you like.

Signs of age and wear are also clues to authentic items. Acquire an eye for patina—the way a piece made of wood, say, or metal changes color as it is exposed to air and light and dirt. Wood also shrinks as it ages and it is soft enough to show tool marks and scars. Look for signs of wear on the arms of chairs, on footrests, around drawer pulls. Iron and steel are harder than wood, but even they show signs of wear: scratches, abrasions, nicks. Check the feet of andirons, trivets, and bootjacks. Authentic scratches are never regular, each is different in width or depth.

The softer metals, such as silver, pewter, or brass, should not only exhibit such scratches but should also have developed rounder contours because they were frequently polished. Glass items will show signs of wear, usually on the bottom where they may have been moved across a dusty surface. Tinned pieces scratch, dent, oxidize, and rust. Look for scratches and dents in logical places, where heavy use would inflict the damage. Rusting and oxidation should be more erratic and not follow any pattern.

Do not hesitate to take any object you're examining to a good source of light. Bright sunlight, a window with a northern exposure, or an unshaded 300-watt bulb should provide sufficient illumination. Some collectors find that a small high-intensity lamp, which they can move back and forth across the surface of an object in a raking motion, is also helpful. Raking light can reveal, for instance, a dip in the surface where an identifying mark may have been removed.

A magnifying glass and a magnet are two other useful tools for collectors. For most people a 5x magnifier is sufficient. There are a variety of styles: some can be attached to your eyeglasses or to a band around your head; others are hand-held. One "flashlight" model comes with a battery-powered light, a good feature if you like to rummage in dark corners. A magnet is essential for anyone who collects metal artifacts.

Technology also provides more sophisticated tools for collectors. Among these, ultraviolet or "black" light is probably the most widely used. You can tell by the way an object "glows" or "fluoresces" under the light if it has any imperfections, if it has been repaired, or if it is a fake. As one collector of early scrimshaw says, the real thing has "a certain glow under a black light. Once you have seen it, it's unmistakable."

Black lights are useful for testing Hummel figures, Doughty birds, dolls, netsuke, and many other objects made of ceramics, painted tin, glass, or ivory. Dealers and auctioneers who specialize in Hummels or other ceramic collectibles often have black lights for your use right on the premises, or you can buy one of your own. Some use batteries; others, electricity. Choose the kind that best suits your needs. (A thorough analysis of various models with a list of suppliers appears in *Maine Antique Digest,* January 1980.)

Collectors can also make use of information provided by the X-ray machine, the microscope, and the spectrograph. Such procedures usually cost money, and the information provided may not seem worth the cost to you. Still, collectors who are considering expensive purchases occasionally want to reinforce their own opinions with scientific evidence.

An X ray can show up many clever repairs; on decoys, for example, putty or an unseen nail will be revealed. A microscopic analysis of a piece of wood from the underside of a desk or table will determine whether the piece was of American or European origin. A spectrogram of a silver bowl reputed to be early American will verify its pedigree.

No one likes to be fooled. But you can't stop buying because you're afraid of making a mistake. Learn all you can. Use your eyes, your hands, and the tools science provides. If you still make a mistake, acknowledge it, keep it somewhere where you'll remember the lesson, and move on to other purchases.

HOW—AND
WHERE—TO BUY

A father once told a daughter: "It takes nerve as well as taste to be a collector." The daughter happened to be Electra Havemeyer Webb, a collector par excellence who eventually accumulated more than 125,000 objects, gathered them all together, and created the Shelburne Museum in Shelburne, Vermont.

That may be an extreme example, but for every collector there comes the moment of truth: the time when you must put your money on the line. Whether you buy from a dealer, at an auction, flea market, or tag sale, that first purchase marks your entry into the world of collecting.

An experienced dealer, who has observed many neophyte collectors, estimates that you can become a "first-class amateur" in three years. It is silly, and probably impossible, for you to spend all that time on the side-lines. Thus you will find yourself doing what other collectors do: learning as you go, getting a feel for objects as you buy.

Before you begin, it is a good idea to figure out how much money you will allot to your hobby. If your funds are unlimited, that is, of course, unnecessary. But most collectors find they are working with a fixed amount of money—either income or capital. If in the beginning you plan to make only small expenditures, you may not need to budget very carefully. But as you progress to higher-priced items, you should have an idea of how much you can allot by the month, by the year, or for each purchase. If you tend to let your enthusiasm carry you away, you may need the discipline of a monthly budget. The yearly plan provides more flexibility; you can buy several objects or save up for one extraordinary purchase.

DEALERS

Most of the antiques and collectibles sold in this country today are sold by dealers. And for the average collector, the dealer is not only the most accessible source for objects he is also the most dependable. An established, knowledgeable dealer is an invaluable resource from whom you can learn much (see pp. 31–32).

There are other advantages, too. When you buy from a dealer, whether in a shop or at a show, you are not likely to be under pressure to make up your mind instantly. Then, too, a dealer preselects for you. Dealers see a lot of merchandise—what their "pickers" bring in, on buying trips, at auctions, at shows—but they buy only what they think their customers will like. You will pay higher prices than if you did the legwork yourself because you benefit from their labors.

You can also get good buys from dealers. If a dealer carries a wide range of objects, and you specialize in, say, fountain pens, she may not know the current value of a Parker Black Giant. You do, so you get a bargain. However, dealers who specialize in one kind of merchandise, such as china or glass, often have to take other items, ephemera, for example, just to get what they want. If you come along at the right time, when they want to unload the "trash," you'll get a bargain.

You may want to patronize a dealer because of the extra services he provides. A dealer may let you take an expensive or unusual piece home and live with it for a few days before you decide to buy. A dealer can put you in touch with craftspeople you may need—weavers or caners, for example. Furniture dealers often do cabinetry work at their own shops. A dealer may let you pay by personal check or credit card, or spread your payments over several months. And, finally, a reputable dealer will vouch for the authenticity of an object.

Naturally such relationships are not without problems. You should know the disadvantages as well as the advantages. Dealers, no matter who they are, are in business to make a profit. They must mark up the items they handle. And some take a heftier markup than others. Some collectors who love the search almost as much as what they ultimately find think dealers get in the way of the excitement. And it's true that having a professional present you with preselected objects removes some spontaneity from collecting. The more knowledgeable you become the safer it is to buy at auction, at flea markets, and from other less orthodox sources. Your knowledge becomes your protection. Advanced collectors usually buy from a combination of sources, trusting their own judgment when they attend auctions or house sales and still maintaining good relationships with dealers they trust.

Finding such a dealer is, of course, the heart of the matter. Dealers have been divided into three categories: the well informed, the ignorant, and the dishonest. One statistic suggests that thirty percent of the country's dealers have been in business fewer than four years. That would be hard to prove, and that fact alone need not be a condemnation. A hobbyist who collected art glass for fifteen years and then decided to become a dealer could still be a knowledgeable, honest businessman. However, the fact remains that there are many dealers in the marketplace who do not know as much as they should—certainly not as much as beginning collectors tend to think they do.

How do you protect yourself? Choose a dealer with the same care that you use in selecting a lawyer or doctor. Ask around. Some museum curators will give you two or three recommendations. Talk to other collectors. Read the ads in antiques publications. Go to shows.

If you feel unsure of your ability to judge a dealer's grasp of the subject, ask a question to which you already know the answer. Then evaluate the answer to see if it's complete, correct—and honest. Beware the dealer who's too positive about dates—"before 1830." Even experts find such judgments tricky; that's why they tend to use so many qualifying words, such as "in the style of."

Notice if the dealer has any reference materials around or mentions them in conversation. One clue to a good dealer is a willingness to refer you to exhibitions, books, magazines, clubs—anything that will increase *your* knowledge of the subject.

Don't let yourself be talked into a purchase. A good dealer should be interested in satisfying you, not just in selling to you. When it comes time to buy, particularly something at a high price, a good dealer should not object if you wish to call in an independent appraiser.

It may seem that you are expecting a lot from a dealer—and you are. But you are hoping for a long-term professional relationship that will be of mutual benefit. In the end your decision may be based on chemistry (you will simply prefer some dealers over others), but if you're wise you will also have checked out the basics.

As you begin to search for a dealer, you'll notice that dealers tend to operate in one of three ways: in shops, at shows, or by mail order. Some dealers manage to combine two or three options. The "shopkeepers" themselves, depending on the kind of merchandise they handle, break down into several categories.

The specialists—those who have concentrated on one area, such as Chinese export porcelain—usually carry only the best quality. Often they operate long-established enterprises; some have been in the same family for generations. Although these shops are not exactly browsing places, don't be intimidated if you are truly interested in the objects for sale. The serious browser is welcome in even the most exclusive stores.

More common—and more comfortable and more fun for most collectors—are the general shops. These dealers carry a variety of merchandise—some old, some not so old; some good, some not so good. They depend on a steady turnover to keep their stock fresh. You may have to look into corners and under tables and you may have to return again and again, but you can find almost anything in one of these shops. In addition the dealers are often willing to shop for you; ask them to keep an eye open for your specialty when they go on their buying trips.

The junk shop or secondhand store is not hard to recognize. The merchandise is unabashedly "used" rather than "old." That's not to say that collectors, especially those who are searching for not so old collectibles, won't occasionally find something they want at these shops. But you should know the odds. Pickers and dealers regularly check out these places; the good items are sifted out, and by and large only the true junk remains.

When you're investigating the shops in your own city or town, you have plenty of time to browse, ask questions, even make return trips. It's not all that difficult to find the shops you like. Finding—and evaluating—antiques shops is somewhat harder when you travel. You can check the Yellow Pages. In large cities there are often "districts" where you'll find many antiques shops. In New Orleans, for example, there are a number of dealers' shops in the French Quarter and along Magazine Street; in New York City, along Madison Avenue, East 57th Street, and Bleecker Street; in Boston, along Charles Street; in San Francisco, along Sutter Street. Shops in small towns can also be clustered. In Hallowell, Maine, for example, look along Water Street. In rural areas shops are naturally more spread out. You can check the advertisements in the trade papers before you leave home. Dealers in some states or regions have banded together to form associations and these groups often publish pamphlets listing members' addresses, specialties, hours, and so forth. Write ahead to the state's chamber of commerce to see if such a listing is available. Once you're in an area, you may be able to pick up a local guidebook or directory.

Some collectors are uncomfortable about buying on vacation. They suspect that prices are inflated during the tourist season. They're often right. But dealers in vacation areas stock more merchandise during their busy months, and you may find objects that just aren't available off-season.

When you're buying far from home, you have to rely on your own common sense and judgment of people. It is more than ever a *caveat emptor* situation. Don't assume that because items are sold from a picturesque barn they are necessarily antiques.

One fairly recent development makes it somewhat easier for collectors to visit a number of shops in a short period of time. The antiques "supermarkets" are clusters of dealers gathered together under one roof. In Hopewell, New Jersey, twenty dealers have opened booths in an old tomato cannery. In Brandon, Vermont, twelve dealers share a barn. Similar operations have opened in many other rural areas and also in large cities.

Antiques shows offer similar advantages. It is probably just those advantages—a wide variety of dealers and objects gathered together in one place—that have increased the popularity of the shows so dramatically.

At the top of the status ladder are the large charity antiques shows held annually in a number of different cities. New York hosts the Winter Antiques Show in January; Houston, the Theta Charity Show in September; Philadelphia, the University Hospital Show in April; and Boston, the Ellis Memorial show in October. These shows attract the most prestigious dealers from around the country. Because the sponsors of these shows are always on the alert for fakes or reproductions, or even for second-rate objects that don't meet the shows' high standards, you can usually be sure of the quality and authenticity of the objects you see. You can also be sure that prices will be on the high side.

Hundreds of other antiques shows are held in armories, auditoriums, civic centers, hotels, and shopping centers around the country. The key to the success of these shows is the management. They set the standards that attract reputable dealers and a buying public. Most of the larger shows feature a variety of items: furniture, decorative arts, paintings, prints. Some specialized shows may offer only regional items or certain kinds of antiques or collectibles, such as Depression glass, or railroadiana, or dolls and miniatures. When you start out on the show circuit, notice the names of the various managers. You'll soon recognize the people who run fine events with reputable dealers and the kind of merchandise you like.

At any show plenty of wheeling and dealing goes on. Even before the doors open the dealers have probably bought and sold dozens of items among themselves. You can't beat that, but you can get there early—the first day if possible—to see the best selection of objects. And plan to take advantage of the many side events—lectures, appraisal sessions, repair services—that show managers are now providing to attract customers.

The third way dealers operate—by mail—will be covered later in the chapter (see pp. 59–61).

DEALING WITH DEALERS

When dealers talk among themselves, they often seem to have as many complaints about customers as customers have about them. They quickly acknowledge that most collectors are friendly, not rude; straightforward, not furtive.

But they do have legitimate complaints. They do not like customers who immediately suspect they're going to be taken. They don't appreciate sotto voce comments about them, their shops, or the quality of their antiques. They don't like customers who lift every lid, wind every clock, tap every compote.

They do not object to serious browsing. They don't mind answering questions; they enjoy it. They don't even object if you walk out without buying anything; that's part of the business. There is some division among them on the subject of negotiating prices. One dealer insists, "My goods are worth what I ask for them. I don't want to haggle." And many dealers, especially those who handle the higher-priced objects, agree. Nevertheless, a few dealers enjoy the give-and-take of bargaining and do not expect a collector to pay the sticker price.

The most tactful and effective way to broach the subject of a lower price is to ask, "Can you do any better?" or "Is that your best price?" Don't discuss the price until you're sure you want to buy. And there's not much sense in asking the best price if you don't know how much you'd be willing to pay. So do your thinking before you approach the dealer.

Dealers routinely give others in the business a discount. Often collectors can get an item at the same price that a dealer would pay. Occasionally they can do better. The dealer's discount can be a percentage of the price or a fixed dollar amount. It may be clearly marked on the price tag or in code. For example: "Quimper plate. $35.00. DO4," translated, means the dealer's price is $4.00 off.

The subject of price codes is a sensitive one. Fewer dealers rely on them now than was true some years ago but they are still occasionally used. A code is a way of pricing items so that the dealer can tell at a glance what the asking price is, but the buyer cannot. Some dealers use only partial codes—stating the price clearly but masking the dealer's discount and their own purchase price. Dealers who use codes defend them because, for one reason, they say, people resent the markup if they sell an object to the dealer and then see it for sale in the shop at a much higher price. But today's collectors prefer clearly marked price tags and, by and large, dealers comply.

Because one of the chief benefits of dealing with a reputable dealer is his willingness to stand behind his merchandise, don't forget to ask for a bill of sale. A simple way to ask: "Would you put all you've told me in writing?" Make sure that the bill is on a proper letterhead or that the dealer is identified by name and address. The item should be fully described: kind of item (tilt-top table); age; provenance; repairs, if any; imperfections, if any. Then ask for the dealer's written guarantee: that if the piece has been misrepresented in any way, your money will be refunded.

You hope there will be no need to use the guarantee. But if you have not taken precautions ahead of time, you will have no legal redress later.

AUCTIONS

In America we will auction almost anything—from livestock to heavy industrial equipment to a painting worth $2 million. We are indeed a nation of auctiongoers, but we are not alone.

Auctions have been around for a long time and have thrived in many different countries. In ancient Rome, for example, one unfortunate Roman fell asleep during the bidding. When he woke up he discovered that every time he had nodded in his sleep he had bought a piece of furniture. In the eighteenth century Samuel Johnson described the behavior of one of his English contemporaries at an auction: He looks "with longing eyes and gloomy countenance on that which he despairs to gain from a rich bidder." Two of the largest international auction houses operating today had their beginnings in London in that century, and auctions in America date to the same period. Records show that in Boston in 1713 a "Publick Vendue" disposed of a collection of books.

There can be little doubt, however, that auctions today reach a greater number of people and handle more merchandise that sells at higher prices than ever before. Sotheby Parke Bernet in New York, for example, reported that for the 1979/80 season their total net sales in North America alone were $248,000,000. Attendance figures at their Madison Avenue gallery reached nearly 300,000. Other auction houses also had a record-breaking year, even if their totals are not so striking as Sotheby's. The season, at least for the large international houses, used to be concentrated in the spring and fall. Now their calendars are full ten months of the year and during some weeks collectors find it difficult to decide which auction to attend.

One fairly recent development, the specialty auction, has become so popular that dealers and collectors plan their trips to New York, New Orleans, or Cape Cod to coincide with one of these auctions. Some of the specialty auctions have become marketing extravaganzas. Sotheby Parke Bernet has had remarkable success with its Collectors' Carrousel: a cluster of specialized auctions of dolls, toys, costumes and clothes, banks, music boxes, and so forth, all scheduled within a few days and all heavily promoted. Often the galleries schedule their auctions at the same time as a major antiques show. January in New York City used to be quiet. Now it's a lively scene because galleries have scheduled auctions while the collectors are in town to attend the Winter Antiques Show.

The activity at the auction houses is due in large measure to the increased numbers of collectors—and their greater sense of confidence in bidding at auction. (Other reasons reflect the galleries' increasing business sophistication, attractive consignment arrangements, extensive promotion, and so forth.)

Auctions will provide you with access to a great range of objects. An auction can contain several hundred lots; only an antiques show gives you an opportunity to see—and handle—such a wide selection of antiques. At some of the larger auction houses attendants are available at presale exhibits to answer questions and give opinions. And, barring an emotional duel, prices are generally lower at auctions than they would be for the same merchandise in a shop. By one estimate prices at auction represent fifty to eighty percent of an item's retail value. The reason behind these figures is that many of the bidders at auctions are dealers, and they must stop bidding at a point where they can add their own markup and still sell the item at a reasonable retail price.

Despite all those attractions auctions tend to be bad places for beginning collectors. The reason is really twofold: buying at auction requires both discipline and knowledge. Only you can provide the discipline. The knowledge comes with experience, but a few observations may help.

The most extraordinary auctions are the glamorous international events held in New York, London, Paris, or St. Moritz, where the bidders dress formally, and the bids on jewelry or furniture or paintings reach into the millions. These are fine spectator events, but for most of us they do not provide much hard experience—or collectible items. The range of auctions accessible to the average collector is still impressive. Fine regional auction houses in many U.S. cities (see the list on pp. 63–64) now hold specialized as well as general auctions (Americana and Victoriana are most popular). In each auction there are likely to be many low-priced items as well as the more publicized higher-priced objects. At Sotheby Parke Bernet two-thirds of the items auctioned last year went for less than $1000.

Below the level of the regional auction houses are other city and suburban auctions that are held on a regular basis and attract a steady group of customers. These second-string houses seldom have top-quality items. But if a first-class object does come up for bids, it will likely sell for less than it might if it were surrounded by other fine objects at a classier auction.

It takes a lot of experience to do well at these auctions. The auctioneers may, or may not, describe an item accurately. There is seldom an informative catalogue; often it is just a mimeographed sheet listing the lots in the order in which they will be sold. Dealers frequent these auctions, looking for unpopular items. One New Yorker who specializes in objects geared to European tastes reports that he finds good buys in New Jersey and Connecticut where such things do not sell well.

Country auctions, like their city cousins, come in various guises. The traditional one-day event where the auctioneer sets up in a front yard and sells off the contents of a house and barn is still popular in rural areas. Other country auctions are held on a regular schedule, for example, every Friday night or Saturday afternoon during the summer months, in a barn, or converted warehouse, or even a tent. Still others are annual fund-raising events sponsored by a local church, hospital, or fire department. There are seldom more than a few good pieces in any of these sales. But the enthusiasm and good spirits of the crowd, combined with the ever-present chance of finding that one good piece, make these events very appealing. Unfortunately, their popularity has spread far and wide, so that prices are occasionally as high as they might be in the city.

MASTERING THE BASICS

The mystique that surrounds auctions, be they in the city or in the country, can be somewhat dispelled by learning the language auction-goers speak. Here is a brief glossary of terms and phrases.

"Against the room," or *"against the floor."* The way an auctioneer accounts for an absentee bid, that is, a bid by mail or phone.

"Against you." Someone else has the high bid.

Bidding. The process of offering ever-increasing amounts of money for an item. Auctioneers usually stick to standard increments in bidding, so that one person must top another's bid by a set amount.

Buyer's premium. A fee (generally ten percent of the top bid) added to the purchase price. This was a controversial subject when Christie's began the system in this country, but it has gradually been adopted by more and more auction houses.

Buy-in. If an item does not meet its reserve—in other words, if no one bids as high as or higher than the reserve figure—the auctioneer will *buy-in* the object for the owner. It is, effectively, withdrawn from sale. The owners pays a small fee to the auctioneer for his handling of the item.

Consignor. The person who brings antiques or collectibles (called *consignments*) to an auctioneer to be sold.

Estate sale. A frequently used word in auction advertising, which means that the objects to be auctioned were all the possessions of one person, now deceased. He or she is often identified. An *estates sale* includes items from a number of people. Reputable auctioneers do not add lots that were not part of the specified estate. An advertisement might read "absolutely no additions." Less scrupulous auctioneers may dilute the sale by adding dealer consignments or their own stock without notifying the public.

"Fair warning." Time is almost up; the auctioneer is about to close the bidding.

Hammer price. The final bid on a lot. Traditionally, an auctioneer raps his gavel or hammer when an item has been sold.

The house. The auctioneer's way of referring to himself or his gallery. There is, for instance, in some galleries a house code. Everything the auctioneer needs to know—the reserve, the presale estimates, any absentee bids—is written in his book in code.

Lot. The object or objects up for bid. A lot can include a pair, a set, or even a group of unrelated items that the auctioneer sees fit to auction together.

Presale exhibition or preview. The time before the auction when you can inspect the items to be sold. For large sales, exhibitions are frequently held the day before; for country auctions it may be only an hour or two before the sale begins.

Provenance. The history of an object, including country or area of origin; previous owners, if known; museum exhibitions, if known.

Pyramid bids. A complex system of mail bidding that adds the amounts allocated for unused bids for early items to the amount available for later bids.

Reserve. The lowest price at which a consignor will allow an item to be sold.

Ring or pool. A group of dealers who conspire to keep the sale price low by not bidding. A designated member of the ring buys the object in the auction and the dealers in the ring then bid among themselves for it.

Spotters. The auctioneer's assistants who are stationed at various points around the floor to help keep an eye on the bidding.

Ten-and-ten. Another way of referring to the buyer's fee. Consignors pay the auctioneer a ten percent commission to sell an item; the buyer pays the hammer price plus an additional ten percent.

Underbidder. The person who makes the next-to-highest bid—she who does not get the lot.

Unreserved or unrestricted. A term that appears in catalogues and in advertisements. It denotes a sale at which no minimum price or reserve has been set on any lot. If neither of these forms appears, you can be almost certain that reserve prices are in effect.

"Yours." You currently have the high bid.

"If you don't go to the preview, don't go to the auction." That advice, from an auctioneer, is the most basic point to remember. (The advice applies only if you intend to bid; auctiongoing can be a spectator sport, too. But beware: it is extremely difficult to remain a spectator. The auctioneer's spiel is designed to entice you into the action.)

Items sold at auction are sold "as is." Although certain limited guarantees are available at some houses, you are in the main dependent on your own sharp eye. So go prepared with tape measure, magnifying glass, magnet, whatever you need. The established auction houses have attendants on duty at the exhibitions. Their job is to open cases, move furniture, unroll rugs, or whatever else is necessary to ensure that potential bidders see an object from every angle. At country auctions you may have to do the pushing and lifting yourself. Take your time in examining the lots that interest you. Make notes. Ask questions. The attendants—at least at the better houses—are knowledgeable. If you wish, you can bring a dealer with you and benefit from his advice. (Whatever financial arrangements you make for this service are between you and the dealer and will depend on the time involved and whether or not you also ask him to bid for you at the auction. If you do, the commission is usually ten percent.)

Besides inspecting the items to be sold, you will also want to find out if there is any admission fee to the auction (there seldom is); if there is a buyer's premium in effect; and if there is a reserve on the items that interest you. Children may not be allowed at either the exhibition or the auction. Ask. Check the conditions of sale. What kind of payment will the house accept? Some will take only cash or traveler's checks; others will accept credit cards or personal checks if the auctioneer's staff knows you. Be sure you know what the requirements are at each house.

Inquire about the procedures for removing any lots you buy. Some galleries insist that all items be removed at the end of the sale. So do the auctioneers who conduct one-day on-site estate sales. Other houses will allow you two to three days; still others will store the item for you until you can arrange transportation. Find out storage charges and what the insurance provisions are. If you cannot provide your own transportation, ask if the auctioneer can suggest a trucker. He usually can. Finally, you will want to find out if any guarantee is in effect. If you do find that age, authenticity, and condition are guaranteed to be as described, you should read the fine print.

If the auction is a catalogue sale, much of this information will be in the catalogue. You may also find presale estimates there. If there is no catalogue, ask the auctioneer or an attendant. You can also ask them for an estimate on when the lots that interest you will come up for sale.

When you arrive at the auction itself depends on your strategy and the amount of time you have. You may prefer to arrive shortly before the objects that interest you will come up for sale. Be sure to allow a safe margin; lots are occasionally sold out of order. Or you can plan to arrive early and stay for the duration of the sale. Bargains often come along before the crowd warms up or after most people grow weary and go home.

If preregistration is required, go first to the desk and sign in. You will be given a numbered paddle or card to identify you when you bid. You may also want to post a refundable deposit before the action begins so you do not miss an important lot while making arrangements during the auction.

Some collectors prefer to stand or sit in the back or on the side so they can spot the dealers (they usually cluster together) and watch all the bidding. Others prefer the front where they can see the lots clearly. Whichever you choose, be sure to select a spot where you can be seen clearly by the auctioneer. As the time comes for you to bid, you may find yourself suffering from acute stage fright. It's perfectly normal. Remembering these things may help.

1. *Understand the order of bidding.* The auctioneer will ask for an opening bid. "May I have a bid of $100 on this Eastlake chair?" If no one responds, he'll gradually drop the level until someone does. Then the bidding proceeds in an established pattern of increments: by $10, say, under $200; by $25 from $200 to $500; by $50 from $500 to $1000. Each auction house sets its own order of bidding. Be sure you know what it is. Also be sure you know if you're bidding on an item, a pair, or the set.

2. *Don't try to be tricky.* To enter the bidding, attract the auctioneer's attention by raising your hand or paddle, or by calling out your bid in a clear voice. You can usually stay in the bidding with as little as a nod. You may have heard about covert signs of bidding—scratching an ear, tugging a lapel, straightening a tie. Bidders do use such secret signals but an auctioneer usually recognizes them as bids only when they come from people he knows or if you have established a code with him before the sale begins.

3. Don't be alarmed if you find you're *bidding against a dealer.* Although it's true that dealers will occasionally "run up" a price for their own reasons, most of them are in business and they must keep their final bid low enough to make a fair profit when they resell. One collector says frankly, "I'm never happier than when I'm bidding against a dealer." And she has a houseful of bargains to prove her point.

4. *Keep your eyes on the auctioneer;* keep your mind alert to the action. Newcomers do occasionally bid against themselves by raising their own bid. Sometimes an auctioneer will tell you that the bid is yours; at other times he may not.

The best bidding strategy is the simplest. Do your thinking ahead of time. You don't have time to deliberate during an auction. Once you've decided what you want, go after it. You probably won't want to display wild enthusiasm, but there's no advantage to hanging back and waiting to be coaxed. Today many people are seeking fine objects, and there will always be competition for the high-quality items. To avoid the dangers of runaway enthusiasm, most veteran auctiongoers advise newcomers to set a top limit and stick to it, whatever happens. That is a good basic rule to follow. On occasion, however, it may pay you to exceed your limit a little. Most people tend to stop bidding at round figures. If you really want the lot, try going up one bid—but only one. You may be surprised to find yourself successful. However, if you discover that the bidding goes quickly past your top price, stay out of the action.

If you are the successful bidder at one of the large auction galleries, an attendant will come to you with a form listing the lot number and sale price. You fill in your name and address. If you're at a smaller house or a country auction, the staff keeps a record by the number on your bidding card or paddle. In either case when you're ready to leave, you go to the desk, give your name or number, and settle your account.

BIDDING BY MAIL

When it is inconvenient to attend an auction in person, collectors can bid in absentia—by mail or occasionally by telephone. Some houses require a deposit before executing a bid; others do not. You can find out at the presale exhibit. If the auction is a catalogue sale, you will usually find a form for order bids in the catalogue. Or you can leave your bid with a house attendant after you inspect the lot. Ask what the presale estimates are and what the order of bidding is at the house. Then write down your top figure.

The house will execute your bid for you, usually by having an attendant call out your bid at the appropriate time. Often the auctioneer himself executes order bids by inserting them into the course of his running commentary. Some auctioneers announce at the start of bidding that they have mail bids to execute; others do not.

If your bid is higher than any in the room, the lot will be yours at the next highest increment, even if that figure is much lower than your order bid. In other words, if you entered an absentee bid of $750 for a Tiffany glass vase, and the bidding, which had proceeded in increments of $50.00, stopped at $550, you would purchase the vase for $600. You would then be notified by mail of the final sale price and given a specific time within which you must make payment and remove the object from the gallery.

Although there is an inherent conflict of interest in allowing an auction house to bid for you, when they have a stake in the sale, most ethical galleries seem to execute order bids fairly. And the procedure is a valuable asset for collectors who cannot attend an auction.

SUBTLETIES

As you attend more and more auctions, you'll begin to notice some of the complexities of the world behind the hammer. In this world dealers are absolutely essential. Without them nothing can function. They are both consignors and buyers. Because dealers must always be on the lookout for fresh stock, they are also constantly selling off items that don't move. One auctioneer reports that when he attends an antiques show, dealers often ask him to stay around until the end of the show: "I'll have a box of things for you to sell, Mike." Collectors, particularly those who specialize and who attend shows as well as auctions, will often recognize certain lots as familiar items they've seen in dealer's shops or booths. That's why there is genuine excitement at an estate sale; fresh items come on to the market.

When dealers are buying instead of selling, they occasionally operate the ring or pool. Because they are conspiring to keep prices down, they do not harm the collector who is bidding against them. In fact the ring is not a bad adversary to have at an auction. The chief sufferer is the consignor who may watch a valuable piece go for a ludicrously small amount. The influx of private collectors into the auction market, however, has helped the consignor. Individual collectors who are interested in an item will bid it up despite the efforts of the pool and, in effect, they then decrease the harm it can do.

But the consignor's chief defense is the reserve—a complicated and controversial subject in itself. The benefits and drawbacks to the consignor are covered on page 97, but there are a few aspects of the practice that are of interest to buyers, too.

Some people become aware of the reserve for the first time when they notice an asterisk or an *R* next to a lot number in a catalogue. Others become confused as they watch the bidding and think the auctioneer is knocking down a lot to an invisible bidder. At other times the auctioneer announces forthrightly that bidding has not reached the reserve and invites further bidding.

These clues point toward a vulnerable area in the auction market.

Reputable people line up on each side of this issue. On the one hand the reserve protects the seller against a disastrous sale. On the other, an unrealistically high reserve results in a buy-in rather than a sale, which is hardly the point of an auction and of benefit to neither consignors nor bidders. One abuse of the system also causes a great deal of anger among dealers and collectors. A consignor who is permitted to place an unrealistically high reserve on, say, a Belter settee, can thereby set a high price level for such settees. Because auctiongoers and collectors assume that the price was paid by a bidder—instead of the owner—other Belter settees are valued higher. It is also possible for the owner then to donate the item to a museum and take a tax deduction at the inflated auction price.

The problem is caused by the secrecy that has surrounded reserves and buy-ins. More and more people are coming to realize, however, that an open market is of benefit to all, and efforts are being made to bring the reserve out into the open where it can be used—but not misused.

Some auction houses, like Richard A. Bourne Co. Inc. in Hyannis, Massachusetts, do not allow reserves. Others will not permit consignors to put a reserve higher than the low of the presale estimate. If an ivory netsuke carried a presale estimate of $300 to $350, then the reserve could not be higher than $300. In New York City the law requires that auction houses identify lots that carry a reserve For example, Sotheby Parke Bernet uses a small square in its catalogue; Christie's uses a dot; William Doyle Galleries, an *R*. Some auctioneers are quite open about telling bidders which items they are buying-in. Most houses no longer include buy-ins in their postsale price lists.

However, the problem is far from solved. Reserves are confusing, misleading, annoying, and, occasionally, dishonest; but they are not about to disappear soon.

FLEA MARKETS

Flea markets have a mixed ancestry—a trace of Turkish, a bit of French, and some English, no doubt. Perhaps the ethnic blend accounts for their exciting, freewheeling atmosphere. More likely, however, their spirit comes from a universal trait: the desire to find a bargain.

The "fleas" do not attract only collectors. Neither do they sell only antiques or collectibles. They sell anything—vegetables, eggs, paper clips, machinery, toys, jewelry, cosmetics—to anybody. You can cook a meal, furnish a house, clothe the family, open an office—all with objects bought at flea markets.

You can also build a fine collection.

For a new collector, however, that same diversity can be a frustration instead of a bonanza. Flea markets are unstructured, sprawling events that are basically the same no matter where you find them. Most flea markets are held outdoors during the warm months. Managers take over an empty lot or field and rent space to dealers who pull up in station wagons, vans, and trucks. They sell directly from their vehicles or from rough tables provided by the management.

A flea market may start off as a one-time event, but if it is successful the managers often continue on a regular weekend schedule. Even flea markets that are fund-raising events for a local charity can follow the same pattern. Some "fleas" have moved indoors and stay open on weekends year-round. Others have grown so large that they have almost taken over a town. The original market in Brimfield, Massachusetts, ran for one day twice a year, in May and September. The town is now the site of numerous markets that stay open for four days, three times a year. In Canton, Texas, the city itself coordinates the activities of the First Monday Trade Days. The market opens the Friday before the first Monday of each month and lasts for four days.

There are two ways a collector can approach a flea market. You can fall in with the spirit of the day and wander casually up and down the aisles looking at everything. If you keep an open mind as you go, you'll certainly find something fascinating. It may, or may not, be what you thought you were looking for.

Or you can follow a more systematic routine. Decide that you are going to search for only two or three kinds of things at this market: a three-drawer oak chest, for example, or objects "Made in Occupied Japan," or a 1920s phonograph. Then, as you go up and down the aisles, your eye will reject everything that doesn't meet your requirements. This method cuts down on the confusion many new collectors feel when faced with literally miles of aisles. And it also makes it possible to "do" a market even if your time is limited.

The first way, of course, leaves you open to serendipity: that marvelous chance encounter between you and a very special thing. But it requires time, patience, and the ability to sift through clutter and come up with treasure.

Whichever technique you use—and you'll probably use both systems at one time or another—here are some ideas that may prove helpful.

1. *Arrive early.* At the Englishtown, New Jersey, flea market, one of the largest, avid collectors arrive before dawn and search out bargains with their flashlights.

2. *Wear comfortable old clothes;* expect mud, dust, and oil-slicked aisles.

3. *Be prepared to buy.* Know the measurements you'll need; bring a tape measure or a folding ruler. Know your background material; bring whatever books, including price guides, you'll need. If you're looking for furniture, bring a van or a pickup, or have some idea of how you'll do the transporting. Bring cash or traveler's checks. If you and the dealer are from the area, you may be able to use a personal check. A few flea market dealers are beginning to accept credit cards, but don't count on using one.

4. *Be prepared to bargain.* Dealers ask what they think the traffic will bear. If you want to pay less, offer less. You may or may not get it at your price but it's always worth the effort. Before you begin bargaining, be sure you know what the item is worth to you, what your top price will be.

5. *Finally, be careful.* Flea markets *are* a great source for bargains. But not everything you see that's cheap is a bargain. It may be a reproduction; it may be repaired. Look it over very carefully.

TAG SALES, HOUSE SALES, AND GARAGE SALES

These days almost anyone can have a house sale—and almost everyone does. Families in transit from one home to another; senior citizens moving to Florida or Arizona; even the third-generation wealthy sell their possessions at tag sales. Sotheby's has conducted house sales in mansions, where the items tagged are likely to be inlaid mahogany tables, enameled Bohemian vases, and large Oriental rugs. At less opulent homes the objects are also less opulent. But there are definitely bargains to be found at house sales.

Tag sale, by the way, is a general term that most people use interchangeably with *house sale, yard sale, garage sale,* and so forth. Although the merchandise at these sales can be as varied as at flea markets, tag sales are held in a home and usually involve just one family's possessions. (Neighborhood sales are becoming quite popular in some states.) The term tag sale is used in a more restricted sense in some parts of the country; then it refers specifically to house sales that are run by professionals.

If you like to play the odds, in other words to look where the rewards will most likely be found, these tag sales are probably your best bet. Most professional tag sales operators will only accept a sale that they estimate will meet a certain minimum total, say, $4000. Therefore, you the customer can be assured of a reasonably large selection of furniture, rugs, lamps, china, silver, glassware—enough to reach that minimum sales total. At other garage sales or yard sales, you may find only the odds and ends of a family's outgrown interests: jigsaw puzzles, ice skates, and decorative flowerpots. Once again, that is not to say that collectibles, especially toys, tools, and kitchen utensils, don't surface at all these sales. They do. It does mean that if your time is limited, you should check into the larger, professionally run tag sales first.

You will find them advertised in the classified pages of the local newspapers. Look under "garage sales" or "household merchandise for sale" or similar headings. Because professional operators depend on a steady following of customers, they will usually identify themselves in the ad.

Read the ads carefully. Note if any of your special interests are listed. "No Prior Sale" means that if an item is advertised it will be there when the sale begins. It also means that you can't knock on the door the day before the sale and try to buy the Oriental rug.

You *can* get there early. At the most popular tag sales the operators distribute numbered cards on a first-come, first-served basis and admittance is based on these numbers. If you get a number somewhere below fifteen or twenty, depending on the size of the house, you will probably be in the first group admitted. Numbers are often distributed hours before the advertised opening time of the sale—at 6:30 A.M. for a 10 o'clock sale. If it's your first time at one of the sales, try to find out in advance what the procedures are.

The competition is fierce in the first few minutes of such sales. Dealers have often captured the low numbers and they make quick decisions. You must be able to do the same. If you are looking for something that was advertised, ask where it is as soon as you enter. Go directly there. If you are looking for your specialty—Lalique or Meissen or Staffordshire—ask for that, too. You can try bargaining if you think an item is priced too high. But it may not work, and you'll have to wait until the last day of the sale when all remaining items are reduced.

Find out what the rules are. Some house sales allow children; most do not. Some operators accept checks; some will hold an item, with a deposit, while you go home for money or arrange transportation. Finally, some allow returns within a few hours; others adhere to a strict "all sales final" policy.

Although all these rules are less stringent at individually run garage sales and yard sales, the procedures are basically the same. Get there early; sometimes it pays to arrive before the advertised hour. Try bargaining. And don't assume that because no professionals are involved the prices will be more reasonable. That may happen. However, it is just as likely that an individual, who is attached to a particular item or does not know its real market value, will set the price too high.

One final note. Be sure you know where the sale is and how to get there. Directions are often omitted or misprinted, and you can lose valuable time if you get lost on your way.

BUYING BY MAIL

Buying by mail can be risky business. What is "mint" or "very fine" to one person may not be "mint" or "very fine" to you.

Because of this risk collectors do not agree on the practice. Some staunchly refuse to buy anything they have not seen. Others—who are perhaps less mobile or interested in a specialty that cannot be found through more regular channels—are willing to take a chance.

There are three prime sources when you buy by mail. First, through *dealers' advertising;* second, through *ads placed by individuals* who may or may not be collectors; and third, through *a "want" ad you place yourself.* Each of these sources can provide important additions to your collection. Each also requires care. Fortunately, there are some precautions you can take to protect yourself.

Dealers who sell by mail advertise regularly in publications such as *Hobbies, The Antique Trader,* and *Collectors News.* The foundation of their business is repeat sales. It pays them to be honest. Still, the burden is on you to be sure that you are getting exactly what was advertised and what you are paying for. Read the advertisements carefully. Note descriptions and qualifying phrases. Some dealers include photographs in the ad; others will send a Polaroid snapshot for a small charge. If the items are keyed to a source book, look them up. Check your price guides—and other advertisements—to be sure the price is fair. If you have any further questions, write, or call, and ask.

Many dealers put the terms of sale in their ads. For example, "Satisfaction guaranteed. Five-day return. Postage and insurance extra." If such information does not appear, ask before you buy. Most dealers allow returns within a specified period. They may also ship items COD or allow you to use MasterCard or Visa cards. A few allow layaways: you pay a certain percentage when you buy and have thirty or sixty days to pay the remainder. These credit arrangements can protect you. So can the return policies. It's a good idea to take advantage of such safeguards until you know from experience that dealers will stand behind their merchandise. Whe you have found reputable dealers in your field, send them a list of your "wants"—items you'd like to buy—and ask them to write to you if they find any.

When you answer an ad placed by a private individual, you are dealing with a different situation. You must still be cautious—perhaps even more so. The owner may not know the true facts about what he is selling. He may not describe it fully or accurately. He may set too high a price. Private collectors do not usually include any terms of sale in their ads. You will have to ask those questions when you answer the ad. Find out as much as you can about the object. Its condition is particularly important because you cannot see it for yourself. Ask specific questions. Are any parts missing? Are there any cracks, chips, or dents? Is it in working order? If you are still unsure, see if a photograph is available. Finally, check on postage and insurance—it's usually extra—as well as the return arrangements.

You should realize that on certain items, particularly something rare or unusual, you are competing against other collectors who have also read the ad. Act quickly. (You can sometimes call instead of writing.) But, unless you are prepared to live with the consequences, do not act carelessly.

The third source for buying by mail—placing your own ad—can be a very creative, if time-consuming, endeavor. The system works particularly well for anyone who is collecting unusual items—Planter's Peanuts memorabilia, Billikin dolls, subminiature cameras. But as the "wanted" columns in trade publications attest, many collectors of more accessible objects like china and silver also find this system effective.

As your first step, select the periodical where you think your ad will be most successful. Consider the merits of a general publication such as *The Antique Trader* versus the more specialized *Depression Glass Daze.* Check out the categories in the publication you choose. Most carry a "Miscellaneous wanted" heading as well as more specific headings such as "Political and military items wanted."

Decide on the size of the ad and the frequency of publication. This will depend on your budget, but as a general rule it's better to run your ad on a regular basis, for, say, six consecutive issues, rather than splurge on one large ad that will run only once. If you can afford a two- or three-inch display ad on a regular basis, by all means go ahead. Most publications publish classified and display rates. If they do not appear, send off a postcard requesting both rates and deadlines.

Compose your ad thoughtfully. Who might have what you want? How can you best reach them? Describe the items briefly. Then add any other phrases, such as "top prices paid" or "state price and condition," that you think will help. Don't be afraid to change your copy if after a short time the ad is not as successful as you had hoped. You may find that a different wording brings a heavier response.

Buying by mail can be an adventure—or a disaster. The key lies in protecting yourself first. Then you can enjoy yourself—and your new acquisitions.

OTHER SOURCES

One of the pleasures of collecting is coming upon that special something when, and where, you least expect it. A collector of weathervanes recalls a handsome rooster he spotted on top of a ramshackle garage in the inner city. One day he saw the garage being torn down. He stopped, offered the owner $90.00, and drove off with his prize. Almost every advanced collector cherishes some similar memory. Buying from unusual sources is a possibility for any collector. It takes imagination, persistence, and a sense of adventure.

One technique that frequently pays off is drawing attention to your own collection. You might, for example, take part in local historical society meetings or offer your collection for an exhibit in a library, a bank, or a school. Or you might consider a display at a trade show or industrial exhibition where people with similar interests, who are not necessarily collectors, might gather. (Be sure, however, that wherever you place your collection, there is sufficient security to protect it. See p. 90.) Your display may attract people with similar objects who are willing to sell them to you.

Another path you might want to try is trading or swapping. This good old-fashioned system can be accomplished in several ways: through swap columns, for example, in some of the down-home magazines, such as *Yankee*. But be cautious; people who advertise in these columns are usually not collectors and may not accurately describe the objects they have to trade.

You may find that trading with other collectors is more profitable. Most collectors' conventions are ideal sites for trading. A new collector who has happened on a rare specimen may want to trade it to an advanced collector for several more common items. A collector can also swap duplicates in his possession or trade-up by exchanging one "fine" specimen for another in "mint" condition.

Never pass up an opportunity to peek into unlikely places such as thrift shops or the attic of a neighbor who welcomes such interest. If you collect ephemera, go to post office auctions, warehouse auctions, military auctions. Try to be around when you hear that a library, a school, or a church is scheduled for demolition or renovation. Lots of paper will go to the junkyard.

Listen. You may pick up clues to new sources from neighbors, storekeepers, or friends. It all comes down to your own creative energies. The more you put into the endeavor, the more you're likely to get out of it.

USING MONEY

The world of antiques and collectibles has traditionally been a cash-and-carry world. Dealers on buying trips traveled the back roads of New England with rolls of bills in their pockets. Those same hefty rolls reappeared at their shops or at shows when they made change for their cash customers. Most auctioneers had cash-only policies. And collectors, afraid of losing an item while they went to the bank, kept large amounts of cash in handy places.

All that has changed in recent years and will probably continue to change as we move further along toward a cashless society. Collectors now have a variety of ways, in addition to cash, to pay for what they buy. Auction houses accept traveler's checks, certified checks, and bank or cashier's checks. They may also accept personal checks, after you establish credit or if you present identification.

In addition to these methods, installment buying is also increasingly available to collectors. Dealers may accept partial payments on large items. You agree to pay a certain amount each month until the armoire or secretary is yours. Some collectors prefer to take out personal bank loans to finance large purchases. Recognized credit cards, such as Visa and MasterCard, are more frequently accepted, even by an occasional auctioneer or flea market dealer.

SOME REGIONAL AND SPECIALIZED AUCTION GALLERIES

Auctions by Theriault
P.O. Box 174
Waverly, Pa. 18471

Barridoff Galleries
242 Middle St.
Portland, Me. 04104

Richard A. Bourne Co. Inc.
Corporation St. P.O. Box 141
Hyannis, Mass. 02647

Butterfield & Butterfield
1244 Sutter St.
San Francisco, Calif. 94109

Chicago Art Galleries
1633 Chicago Ave.
Evanston, Ill. 60201

Christie's
502 Park Ave.
New York, N.Y. 10022
  Christie's East
  219 East 67th St.
  New York, N.Y. 10021

William Doyle Galleries
175 East 87th St.
New York, N.Y. 10028

Du Mouchelle Art Galleries
409 East Jefferson Ave.
Detroit, Mich. 48226

Samuel T. Freeman & Co.
1808-10 Chestnut St.
Philadelphia, Pa. 19103

Garth's Auctions
2690 Stratford Road Box 315
Delaware, Ohio 43015

Milwaukee Auction Galleries
4747 West Bradley Rd.
Milwaukee, Wis. 53223

Morton's Auction Exchange
643 Magazine St. Box 30380
New Orleans, La. 70190

Phillips
867 Madison Ave.
New York, N.Y. 10021
  525 East 72nd St.
  New York, N.Y. 10021

Plaza Art Galleries
406 East 79th St.
New York, N.Y. 10021

Robert W. Skinner
Route 117
Bolton, Mass. 01740
  585 Boylston St.
  Copley Square
  Boston, Mass. 02116

C. G. Sloan & Co.
715 13th St. N.W.
Washington, D.C. 20005

Sotheby Parke Bernet
980 Madison Ave.
New York, N.Y. 10021
  Sotheby's York
  1334 York Ave
  New York, N.Y. 10021
  7660 Beverly Blvd.
  Los Angeles, Calif. 90036

Adam A. Weschler & Sons
905-9 E Street N.W.
Washington, D.C. 20004

Richard W. Withington
Hillsboro, N.H. 03244

DISPLAYING AND PRESERVING

Never has so much old paint been scraped off so much old furniture in order, as collectors said, "to get down to the original wood." . . . Early American hand-blocked wallpapers were copied for machine production and sold by the mile. There was a boom in hand-hooked rugs. . . . Primitive paintings, especially of farm scenes and dour ancestors in black suits or black bonnets . . . were hung over fireplaces in suburban homes. Prints that Currier & Ives had sold for a quarter were handsomely framed in curly or bird's-eye maple. . . . Rogers groups again stood on little living-room tables.

From the internal evidence one might assume that this is a description of the 1960s and 1970s. But it is not. The period is the 1920s and the facts were presented by Russell Lynes in his book, *The Tastemakers*. Lynes attributes this revival of interest in early American antiques to the opening of the American Wing of The Metropolitan Museum of Art in 1924.

In the 1920s, too, collectors came from all age groups. They were both rich and middle-class, suburban and urban. Then, as now, decorators advised the public to use their own taste, to be individuals. In 1930

Emily Post published *The Personality of a House,* in which she suggested that "its personality should express your personality." Her dictum has its echoes in today's eclectic style, in which collectors boldly mix antiques with contemporary, the fine with the not so fine, Chinese with American with French.

To many observers our determined search for individuality in our homes is actually part of a broader rebellion against the mass-produced environment we now inhabit. Antiques and collectibles add warmth and character to a home. They indicate the personality of the people who live there and provide a surprising, charming, or even a humorous note wherever they're placed. A stark white room sparsely furnished with Mies chairs, stainless steel tables, and track lighting becomes a uniquely personal environment when a collection of old toys and some eighteenth-century country furniture are added. A rather ordinary family room becomes a special place when a group of cigar-store Indians and a collection of advertising signs are added.

There are no rigid rules to follow in arranging antiques and collectibles—at least none that cannot be broken successfully. But certain aesthetic principles and practical considerations do apply. How collectors make use of their environments, each with its own peculiar blend of advantages and disadvantages, will determine how successful they are at displaying their treasures. A fine piece can appear mediocre if it is not effectively presented, if it is out of scale with its surroundings, or if it is denied the space it needs to be appreciated.

One of the first problems a collector must confront is the appearance of clutter, a situation one decorator describes as "too many busy children all competing for attention." The issue is a point of frequent discussion between one pair of collectors. He would have everything—baskets, cloisonné, Staffordshire dogs, and Kentucky rifles—on display. She, believing that less is more, doesn't want to cover every surface.

There can be only individual answers to this dilemma. Depending on the kinds of objects you collect, the size of your home, and your lifestyle, you can probably find ways to display your collection tastefully and effectively. But it may not be easy and it will take time. Pieces will come and go until you find the right mix—a fine object beautifully displayed.

You may have to put some objects out of sight, which you can do temporarily, then bring them out and put others away. There are hidden benefits to this system: your home always looks different, and you always have a fresh supply of anecdotes to tell. Collectors agree that a large part of the pleasure of displaying their antiques is the opportunity to tell the story behind an object.

For some people the issue of storage versus display arises even before they become collectors. One woman credits her interest in miniatures to the time she visited a doll collector's home. As she recalls, "Every single doll was packed away in a box, carefully labeled and preserved. But there was no way to enjoy them every day. I decided then and there that if I ever became a collector I'd find something small enough to keep on display. I have all my miniatures in glass cabinets in the living room. There's no dusting and I can look at them every day."

The dilemma is not unique to collectors of modest means. One wealthy couple who could not tolerate the idea of storing any of their many fine paintings had their architect design sliding panels for their home. Although some paintings are out of view temporarily, they are easily retrieved by sliding the panels back and forth.

A guiding principle that can turn clutter into harmony is *keep a collection together.* Seen as a group, even the most ordinary objects take on interest and drama. When a collection of silver Art Deco picture frames is placed on one large tabletop, the result is impressive. If they were scattered about on various tables, shelves, and mantels, the effect would be lost.

You can occasionally make an exception to this rule. If you collect large items, quilts, for example, each can still make a dramatic statement on its own. And, of course, if you collect furniture, it makes no sense to group all your tables or desks or chests together.

Furniture presents problems and solutions of its own. These days very few people try to create period rooms, such as an entire eighteenth-century bedroom or a Victorian parlor. Most collectors prefer to buy pieces they like, whatever the style or period, and put them together in a careful blend.

Achieving such a blend takes time. Line, shape, and scale become very important. Try to select pieces that are flexible, that you can use in various ways in various rooms. New homes are not so large as earlier ones; buy pieces that will not overwhelm your rooms.

Some collectors insist on using their antiques only in the way they were originally intended: chairs as chairs, desk as desks, teapots as teapots. In many cases, however, such a goal is out of the question. Spittoons and inkwells do not fit in with current habits. Weathervanes no longer preside over the countryside; they've moved inside to be displayed as sculptural objects.

However, a general principle remains: if you want to use an antique for something other than what was originally intended, try not to destroy its integrity. Don't turn a handsome rifle into a standing lamp. And never tamper with a truly fine piece, one that should be preserved intact as a tribute to its own time.

A final consideration for collectors who specialize in furniture is basic practicality. Will the arrangement work for your family? When John D. Rockefeller, Jr., arranged furniture in Bassett Hall, once his home but now a part of Colonial Williamsburg, in Williamsburg, Virginia, he would ask a knowledgeable friend to come over and help him assess the results. "You be the host," Rockefeller would say, "and I'll be the guest and we'll see how this feels." You can play the same game. Think about traffic patterns and amenities such as ashtrays, coasters, and lamps. A room should look good but *be* comfortable.

WHERE TO DISPLAY COLLECTIONS

The average home, no matter how small, offers many places to display a collection. It may help if you think in terms of focal points. A collection should form an artistic composition, a still life that creates strong dramatic interest in one corner or one area of a room.

You can display collectibles of almost infinite variety on a wall. Oil paintings, watercolors, posters, photographs, prints, mirrors, and maps are obvious choices, but collectors also hang plates, clocks, quilts, slaw cutters, cookie cutters, keys, cups, and porringers on their walls.

Once again try not to scatter the collection around the room. A grouping of many similar objects makes a contribution instead of creating a distraction. The grouping as a whole needs space around it, and each item within the arrangement should have enough space to make its own statement.

A traditional guideline says that at least one side of a grouping should form a straight line. You can follow the line of an architectural element, such as a window, a door, a stairway, or a mantel, or of a piece of furniture, such as a desk or a sofa. Although this kind of arrangement does ensure harmony, many collectors have successfully put together asymmetrical displays. The late Peggy Guggenheim hung more than 100 pairs of earrings on her bedroom wall in a free-form grouping that was both dramatic and orderly.

Depending on your collection, you may prefer to use shelves instead of hanging objects directly on the walls. Shelving also gives you an opportunity to incorporate other decorating techniques. You can, for example, place a mirror behind the shelves to reflect and enhance your collectibles. You can, if you like, choose Lucite or glass units so that the cases seem to disappear and the antiques alone become the focal point. If all the items in your collection are of a similar size and shape, you can place certain pieces on pedestals or stands to highlight them and add variety to the display.

Many collections look best—and are safest—when displayed in cabinets, cupboards, shadowboxes, and other similar enclosed units. Only you can decide the kind of case that will look best. Some collectors try to display objects in a cabinet of the same period as their antiques. But that is probably too restrictive for most people. You leave yourself more options if you also consider altering an already damaged or "married" cupboard to suit your needs or having cabinets custom-made to your specifications. Shadowboxes can be fashioned from old picture frames or clock cases, or bought ready-made. Once again, rely on basic aesthetic principles—harmony, scale, and design—to help you select the proper case for your collection and your home.

Many of the open surfaces of your home—mantels, windowseats, and the tops of chests and desks—can also provide highly visible places for prized collections. Boxes, books, decoys, and candlesticks, to name just a very few examples, can be effectively displayed in this way.

Consider stairways, doorways, halls, alcoves, foyers, windows, and ceilings as potential places to display your antiques or collectibles. Don't be afraid to move things around. One collector says she gets her best ideas at night and she cannot wait until morning to try them out. She has been known to rearrange fifty fairy lamps at 2:00 A.M. Another collector discovered that her rambunctious family could not stay clear of the baskets she'd arranged on the stairs. The baskets now hang from the ceiling of her breakfast room.

As you work at arranging—and rearranging—your collection, keep in mind that three components, *space, color,* and *lighting,* vitally affect the results of your effort.

We become most acutely aware of *space* when it's lacking. An over-crowded display of Hummels can destroy the charm of each. A group of dolls crammed shoulder to shoulder does not give the viewer an oppor-tunity to confront any one doll eye to eye and appreciate its singular beauty.

Collectors who have grasped this principle know that space is all but tangible. They are aware of the movement of the eye as it travels around a room taking in one object after another and they count on this move-ment to enhance their display. Each object in a collection, whether it's on a shelf, in a cabinet, or freestanding, should be surrounded by enough space so that it can be seen and appreciated without distraction.

Color, the second of these components, can often be used to create the effect of space. It can unify a wall or a room, providing either a dramatic or a muted background for the collection. Some collectors select a color or colors drawn from the objects themselves—onionware displayed in a blue and white kitchen. Others choose a color that offsets the collec-tion—Worcester figurines displayed against a dark brown wall.

Color can bring out the patina in wood, the opalescence in glass, and the texture in woven objects. It can serve as a fine backdrop for oil paintings. Only when you are aware of the many purposes color serves, can you use it effectively.

The same is true for *lighting.* The right source of light not only en-hances a collection but also creates whatever mood you want. Collectors use a variety of techniques to create a variety of effects. One collector of folk art portraits finds picture lights and spotlights inconsistent with the paintings and with the eighteenth-century farmhouse in which he lives. His home has a gracious rural atmosphere in which guests often view his paintings by candlelight.

Others find that their objects show off best in daylight. Diffused or indirect daylight is fine in most cases. The sun, however, is not an ideal source of light for many collectibles. The heat and the ultraviolet rays can do damage to watercolors, textiles, wood, all paper collectibles, even colored glass. If you want to display valuable items in or near windows, as the Sandwich Glass Museum in Massachusetts does, you should also follow their example and install sheets of Plexiglas over the windows.

The Plexiglas screens out the ultraviolet rays. You preserve the aesthetic effect of sunlight but prevent the damage it can cause.

When you want to dramatize certain items in a room, you can make good use of hidden spotlights or of track lighting. Before you make a final decision, try out several possibilities by shining a desk lamp or a flashlight from different places. Consider whether the lines of the object are emphasized or lost, whether the colors stay true or are distorted, whether shadows enhance or detract from the effect.

For items displayed in cabinets, recessed lighting is effective. Keep the lights out of view and at a safe distance from the objects. Lights in confined spaces can generate a surprising amount of heat.

PRESERVING YOUR COLLECTION

There is no question that preventive medicine is best. In other words if you are aware of the problems that can arise *before* they arise, you will do better than if you wait and then try to repair any damage that occurs.

Sensible precautions begin while you are choosing a place to display your collection. Don't place fine old furniture near sunny windows or any other source of heat. The wood will warp and dry out. Many people succumb to the temptation to hang a favorite oil painting over the fireplace, traditionally the focal point in a room. But that can, in fact, be the most dangerous place for a painting. It is exposed not only to the drying heat of the fire but also to soot and grime.

All artworks deserve the best of care. Carry a painting by placing one hand at the top of the frame and one hand underneath. When you lay it down, rest it on a surface that is large enough to support the entire frame. Never lean paintings one against another. Whenever you're hanging, be sure that the materials you use—nails, wire, hooks, Velcro strips—are designed to hold the weight of the objects. And after they're on the wall, check periodically to be sure the fastenings are still secure.

Antiques displayed in cabinets or cupboards require other precautions. Check glass or wood shelves to be sure they will support the weight of your collection. Place objects well back from the edge of a shelf. Repeated vibrations, common in every home, can slowly nudge a prized item over the edge. If you like to display plates or platters upright, use easels or plate holders. Some collectors prefer to make a deep groove in the shelf or attach a piece of molding to it to prevent the lower edge of a plate from sliding. Don't hang cups by their handles.

Objects displayed on tabletops are perhaps most vulnerable. You can prevent scratches on a valuable table and the base of a rare figurine by affixing a piece of felt to the bottom of the figurine. Florist's clay, a safe gumlike substance that adheres to any object, will keep a breakable item attached to its shelf or table. You can also use the clay to keep lids securely fastened to jars or crocks or tureens.

Don't put treasured items in the path of heavy traffic. When you're having a party, move fragile pieces to the tops of cabinets or into corners where elbows won't jostle them.

If you collect silver, china, or glassware that was once used at the table and you'd like to use it, too, go ahead. But remove food or liquids as soon after the meal as possible. Although some collectibles, such as Depression glass, can be placed in the dishwasher without danger, most cannot. To be safe, don't take a chance.

ORDINARY CARE

When you must wash antiques or collectibles, use lukewarm water and a mild detergent. Some curators recommend that you do not immerse old glass at all but merely wipe it with a cloth dampened in the detergent solution and then dry it thoroughly. Follow the same procedure for unglazed porous ceramic pieces.

You can immerse porcelain or stoneware pieces that have glazed nonporous surfaces. Be sure to rinse them to remove all traces of the detergent. Never use an abrasive cleaner or scouring pad on any fine object. If you must remove a stubborn stain, ask the advice of an expert. There are several remedies that work well, but each has a different purpose and requires a different set of instructions.

Many collectors place a soft towel at the bottom of the sink while they're working. They find it prevents accidental chips and cracks on delicate pieces. If you can move your faucet to the side while you wash, do that, too. Never clean fragile objects when you're tired or rushed.

If your collection includes metal objects—brass, copper, silver, pewter, tin, iron—detergent and water are obviously not the answers to your cleaning problems. Metals react to their environment in a variety of ways; they can tarnish or rust or pit or scratch. After a time old metals also develop a patina, a glow that few collectors would willingly destroy. The objective, then, is to find a nonabrasive cleaner that will restore luster to the pieces but not destroy the patina.

You'll have to select from among dozens of polishes and cleaners now on the market. Ideally, you will not use any product that you or someone you respect has not used and found satisfactory. But that is not always possible. So whenever you try a new polish or cleaner, read the label carefully. Follow instructions. Test a small area first to be sure the cleaner is not too harsh for your metal. Don't rub too hard; you can remove the finish as well as the tarnish. And don't use hard-bristle brushes to clean in crevices or designs. For brass, bronze, and copper that have been lacquered, you do not need to polish at all. Simply dust or wipe clean with a dampened cloth.

Caring for old furniture requires, first, that you know the kind of wood you have and, second, that you know which, among the many products available, will achieve the results you want. Unsealed woods should be rubbed with an oil, such as lemon oil, to keep them from drying out. A paste wax, like Butcher's wax, should be used to clean and protect all other woods. As a general rule, dust frequently, but wax infrequently. Whatever product you use, the secret lies in the rubbing. One curator dryly suggests that you try to remove more polish than you put on.

When you dust, especially painted pieces or those with inlaid designs, be sure your cloth is clean, soft, and free from loose threads that could catch and pull up a sliver of wood.

Antiques and collectibles made of fabric are difficult to dust. Some can be vacuumed; others washed or dry-cleaned. Textiles are also endangered by sunlight, excessive dampness, and pests such as moths and carpet beetles. The best solutions to these problems are preventive: keep textiles clean, dry, and away from direct sources of light, whether they are on display or in storage.

Paper collectibles, rightly called ephemera because of their fragile nature, require the same kind of sensible care that textiles do. Heat and light will make the paper brittle or yellow; moisture can cause a fungus growth. Dust and common pollutants can also damage old paper.

If you decide to mat or frame any of your paper collectibles, you can do the work yourself or give the job to a reputable framer. In either case be sure you know the proper procedures to be followed. You should, for instance, use only acid-free materials for matting. Four-ply 100 percent rag board, which is occasionally called museum board, is the best choice. If you're in doubt about the best products or methods, check with dealers, other collectors, or one of the specialized reference books written specifically for paper collectibles.

RESTORING AND REPAIRING

No matter how careful you are, there may come a time when you will have to take further measures to keep your collection at its best. You may want to restore or repair.

The most important rule to remember is *never do anything unless you're absolutely sure you know what the results will be.* It may seem a simple task to repaint, refinish, or reweave one of your collectibles. But specialists are unanimous in warning that amateurs should not attempt operations like these without taking certain precautions.

Consider the object. If it is very old or very rare, you would be wiser to leave the task to a professional. Only an expert should clean a fine oil painting, restore an Oriental rug, or reupholster an eighteenth-century wing chair.

If, on objects of lesser value, you want to do the work yourself, ask for advice from museum curators, dealers, and other collectors. Consult reference books (see the bibliography for some general works; more specific handbooks are available in certain fields). Any advice you receive will most likely be tempered with the warning that each object has its own peculiarities and that general rules often have to be modified for different situations. To complicate matters, the experts do not always agree on procedures. New discoveries sometimes make old methods obsolete; at other times they reinforce the traditional techniques.

Proceed, then, with caution. Weigh all the advice you receive. Practice your skills on lesser objects. When you do tackle a good piece, start working on an inconspicuous area. And if the results don't seem to be all you think they should be, don't be afraid to stop and turn the job over to a professional.

Your other alternative, of course, is to leave the piece unrestored or unrepaired. And, for objects that are not in danger of falling apart, this is the course an increasing number of collectors seem to prefer.

PROTECTING YOUR COLLECTION

While you are engrossed in adding to your collection and displaying it tastefully, your thoughts may not often turn to more prosaic matters, such as record keeping, insurance, smoke detectors, or burglar alarms. Unfortunately, problems do arise, and any loss, no matter how small, can be quite a blow. Most collectors speak first of the emotional distress they would feel. How could I ever replace what I have spent years collecting? But in today's market, financial losses can be equally disturbing. Only a very few people can afford to shrug off the money they've invested in their antiques or collectibles.

For most of us the loss of valued objects means that money may not be available for a replacement at today's prices or, at best, that it must be siphoned from some other investment or planned purchase. Protecting your collection may seem tedious, but it makes very good sense.

RECORD KEEPING

Begin by setting up a simple record-keeping procedure that you will be able to follow without much effort. The easier the system, the more likely you are to keep it up-to-date. Your solution will depend on the size, the complexity, and the value of your collection. Forty paintings from the Hudson River school would quite properly require more documentation than forty charming, but less valuable, figurines like "snow babies."

At the very least you should have an up-to-date inventory list, complete with the prices you paid and current market values. This can be done quite simply on sheets of lined paper. List the objects in the collection in one column on the left. Draw a second narrow column for the purchase price. Leave plenty of space to the right to allow for notations showing changes in market prices. Be sure to date every entry. If you are actively buying and selling objects, you may also want to include a column noting when a piece was sold and at what price. The primary objective of the inventory list, however, is to establish what you own at a given time and how much each item is worth.

There are several other filing systems that collectors can use. One woman makes her notations on index cards and keeps those, together with receipts, appraisals, and other valuable documents, in a series of shoe boxes. She identifies the contents of each box by object and year. You may prefer to use Manila folders. Organize them by item, category, or year. Place copies of articles about your specialty, along with bills of sale, auction catalogues, and so forth, in appropriate folders. Or you can make use of ring binders filled with pages covered by plastic sleeves, into which photographs or documents can be placed. The binders will hold a variety of materials and you can add pages as necessary.

What kinds of records should you keep? Your files will naturally vary with the kind of objects you collect, but there are some broad categories from which every collector draws material.

1. *Purchases.* If you bought from a dealer, the bill of sale will show the date, the price you paid, the sales tax, if any, and may include the dealer's guarantee. It is an important piece of paper to keep.

   If you bought at auction, keep the catalogue description, if there was one, and your receipt. Be sure to make a note of the date, the object, and the purchase price if the gallery didn't.

   If you bought through an advertisement, keep a copy of the ad, a copy of all correspondence about the object, a record of telephone calls, shipping charges, and insurance. This information will help you set a fair price if you decide to sell and may also provide deductible expenses for your income tax return if you sell at a profit.

2. *Supporting information.* Keep copies of advertisements offering similar objects, price guides, auction catalogues, articles that appear in magazines, newspapers, or books—anything you read that will enhance the value of your antiques and support your own records. Be sure the files are safe and easily accessible for appraisals and insurance. You will also find up-to-date background files essential for setting a fair price when you sell.

3. *Appraisals and insurance.* Both of these areas are important elements in your record keeping and are described in detail later in this chapter.

4. *Sales.* Keep records of or receipts for all expenses incurred in the sale—advertisements, telephone calls, postage, travel. These may also be deductible items on your income tax if you make a profit on the sale.

To all these records add photographs. You'll find that good clear photographs of every object in a collection serve many purposes. You can use them to identify the objects you have or to support insurance claims in case of loss. If you're looking for a buyer, you can carry pictures with you more easily than the objects themselves. You can send photographs to auction galleries for free appraisals and to Question and Answer columnists for further information. You can bring them with you to conventions, flea markets, swap meets, wherever collectors gather.

You do not have to be a professional photographer to take adequate snapshots of antiques or collectibles. (If you are looking for artistic photographs—the kind that could be framed or used for illustrations in a book—you do need a professional. Still photography is an art; it requires both skill and the right equipment.)

For the kind of pictures you want for your files, you can use almost any equipment—a pocket camera such as the Kodak Instamatic, any 35mm, or even a Polaroid. The advantage of a Polaroid is, of course, that you see the results immediately. You can then move objects, change the background or the lighting, to achieve better results.

A few basic rules will help you take good pictures.

1. *Don't try to put too many objects in one photograph.* If you can, take each item individually. If you can't, keep each grouping to a maximum of four objects, no matter what their size. Move in as close as you can; try to fill the frame with the object.

2. *Arrange the objects so that each can be seen* as fully as possible. If markings are important, as they are on plates, for example, take both front and back views.

3. *Use a plain, contrasting background.* Black is best for glass. But you can use any color for other objects, as long as the background doesn't compete with the design or the decoration on the object itself.

4. *Place a ruler or yardstick in the picture for reference if size is important,* as it is on miniatures.

5. *Shoot straight on if you can;* this will minimize distortion. If you are shooting an object with a shiny surface or one covered with glass, you can try taking the picture at a forty-five-degree angle or you can cover your flash with a white handkerchief to reduce the glare. The handkerchief technique also helps avoid glare if you want to move in closer than the flash range recommended for your camera.

6. *Lighting can be a problem* and you may have to try different techniques—flash, existing light, daylight—with different film until you come up with a satisfactory solution.

   You may be able to avoid the issue entirely if you can photograph your collection outdoors. Select your background as carefully as you would indoors and check shadows before you shoot. Sunny days often bring deep shadows; overcast days or open shade can provide soft even lighting, which is excellent for certain close-ups.

7. *Use black-and-white or color film, depending on your collection.* Lacy sandwich glass would look fine in black and white; carnival glass would lose much of its charm. There is a wide variety of fast color and black-and-white film available. Ask at a camera store for guidance in selecting the best film for your camera and your purpose.

8. *Be sure to complete your records by dating the photograph and describing the object completely:* size, condition, maker, and so forth.

Keep the photographs with your other files, in the shoe boxes, folders, or ring binders. Many collectors keep one set of photographs at home and another set (or the negatives) in their safe-deposit box. This is, in fact, an excellent practice for other valuable records as well. Make copies of your inventory list, appraisals, and bills of sale, and put the originals in the safe-deposit box. Keep the copies at home for easy reference.

APPRAISALS

An appraisal is, in the simplest terms, an attempt to set a value on an object or group of objects. You can, and probably do, make your own appraisals. As you attend auctions and flea markets, wander through antiques supermarkets, read catalogues, ads, and price guides, you may come upon objects similar to those in your collection. If you make a note of these comparable prices, you will have a good idea what your own collection is worth in the current market. (This procedure requires some self-discipline. You cannot assign a similar value to your Doughty birds, for example, if they are not in as fine condition as the ones sold at auction.)

The more knowledgeable and active a collector you are, the more accurate your own appraisals will be. Such an effort is certainly worthwhile for most antiques and collectibles. At the very least it satisfies your curiosity, reaffirms your good judgment, and provides essential information for both buying and selling.

There are several situations, however, when you may find it helpful, even necessary, to use a professional appraiser.

1. *For insurance.* Some companies require an appraisal before they will issue a fine arts policy on your collection (see pp. 83–87).

2. *For tax purposes.* If you are donating an object to a museum and planning to take a tax deduction for the gift (see pp. 107–108), the Internal Revenue Service usually requires an appraisal to establish the fair market value of the gift. If you inherit an estate, an appraiser must go over the items you inherit to establish their taxable value. If you are planning to dispose of your own estate, an appraiser can help you ascertain its value.

3. *When buying.* Collectors who are interested in a very fine or very expensive antique occasionally feel more comfortable with their decision when an independent appraiser assesses the item and finds the asking price is in line with market values.

4. *When selling.* An appraiser can often guide you in establishing prices at which to sell certain antiques. This can be particularly helpful if you have held an object for many years and can't guess at its current value, if you're mystified by an object, or if it's extremely rare or valuable. Once an appraiser gives you an opinion of fair market value, however, you cannot assume you will receive that amount when you sell. Most antiques and collectibles are sold at prices that are below current market values.

An appraiser is, ideally, an independent figure who has no personal interest in the object being evaluated. In addition, the professional appraiser should bring knowledge, experience, and integrity to the assignment.

Unfortunately, such qualifications are far from universal. The profession is growing rapidly to meet the demands made by museums, banks, insurance companies, and collectors themselves. But there are no uniform licensing procedures and almost anyone can be an appraiser. Once again collectors find themselves in a *caveat emptor* situation. They must protect themselves from the well meaning but uninformed as well as from the more unscrupulous who see no reason to learn the antiques business before setting themselves up as appraisers and charging for their services.

It takes years of experience to become a skilled appraiser. Such a person is well worth the fee. But how do you find a qualified appraiser?

You can start with the two major associations, both of which publish directories of their members. The Appraisers Association of America, 60 East 42nd Street, New York, New York 10165, charges $3.00 for a current directory. The American Society of Appraisers, P.O. Box 17265, Washington, D.C. 20041, does not charge for its directory. Members and senior members of ASA must pass special written and oral examinations.

The primary drawback of the associations is their geographical limitation. Each organization counts its membership in the hundreds. The ASA, for example, lists only two appraisers in Massachusetts, two in North Carolina and two in Indiana. Even other states, which have greater representation, do not have coverage in all specialties. If there is no ASA or AAA member in your area, you will have to look elsewhere.

You can ask for references from a local museum. Curators often know who's qualified in their particular specialties. You can also check with the trust department of your bank, with auction galleries, with other collectors, and with dealers.

Many dealers are, in fact, appraisers, too. And if a dealer specializes in the same field—be it pre-Columbian art or textiles or architectural items—he can be a highly qualified appraiser for your collection. Certainly he should be aware of market values.

You should be sure, however, that a dealer-appraiser is truly a disinterested party. There can be an inherent conflict of interest when a dealer acts as an appraiser. The dealer, knowing that he may want to buy the collection in the future, may deliberately submit a low appraisal to set the stage for his later offer. Honest appraisers deplore this tactic. As the ASA observes, "Anyone using an appraisal made by an appraiser who has an interest or a contemplated future interest in the property appraised might well suspect that the report was biased and self-serving and, therefore, that the findings were invalid."

And the association declares that it is "unethical and unprofessional for an appraiser to accept an assignment to appraise a property in which he has an interest or a contemplated future interest."

Most experienced appraisers accept this standard and will include "a statement of disinterest" in their report.

As you search for an appraiser, keep in mind that you are looking for someone with knowledge, experience, and integrity. When you find someone you think may meet your standards, question her carefully. Ask about her previous clients. Has she done any work for museums? Try to find out her specialties—without revealing your own. Ask what will be included in the written appraisal. An appraisal, especially one that must be filed with the IRS, should contain:

1. A summary of the appraiser's qualifications, with emphasis on how they relate to this assignment.
2. A complete description of each object to be valued.
3. A statement of the value of each object and the appraiser's definition of the kind of value obtained, that is, "replacement value" or "fair market value."

   If, for instance, you hire an appraiser to evaluate your collection for insurance purposes, she should quite properly place a high valuation on the items because she must determine replacement value, the highest price you might have to pay to buy similar items. But, should you decide to donate the collection to a museum, the appraiser must come up with the fair market value: a figure that the IRS says represents the price at which property would change hands between willing buyers and willing sellers, neither being under any compulsion to buy or sell, and both having reasonable knowledge of relevant facts. This figure may well be lower than "replacement value," depending on the quality and rarity of the object.

When an appraisal is done to determine estate taxes, many owners hope for a low appraisal, with values that might be reflected in a distress or liquidation sale. That would, they believe, lower their taxes on the estate. However, the IRS is understandably suspicious in such situations, and it is risky business to expect unrealistically low appraisals to pass inspection. (It may, in addition, be shortsighted. If you then decide to sell certain parts of the collection that received a low evaluation, you are subject to higher capital gains taxes when you sell at a fair market price.)

4. The basis upon which the appraisal was made. One acceptable method of evaluation is based on the sale price of comparable objects. If the appraiser uses this system, items chosen for comparison should be truly similar to those in your collection.

5. The date the property was valued.

6. The signature of the appraiser and the date the appraisal was made. Appraisals should be made as close to the date of valuation as possible.

7. A statement of disinterest such as, "I hereby declare I have no undisclosed interest in the objects below."

Ask, finally, how the appraiser will determine her fee. There are three different methods. One is the *flat fee,* a system used by many appraisers as well as some auction galleries, such as Sotheby Parke Bernet. SPB says its rate is determined by the number of experts required, the complexity and size of the collection, and the amount of time the staff must spend on the appraisal. Travel time is not included. One advantage of allowing auction galleries to do your appraisal is that they will often refund the entire fee or rebate part of it if you consign the collection to them within a certain period of time.

Appraisers also charge *by the hour or by the day*. Rates vary widely, depending on the region and the experience of the appraiser.

The third method is to determine the fee by charging *a percentage of the appraised value*. Be sure that if your appraiser uses this system, the percentages go down as the valuation goes up. In other words, the fee on an appraisal totaling $50,000 or less might be 1½ percent. However, if the valuation were to go above $50,000, the percentage should go down to perhaps 1 percent. Whatever the method, an appraiser should willingly reveal her fee to you. And you should reach an agreement on the fee before you give her the assignment.

Once you have selected an appraiser, cooperate with her. Show her your records, including bills of sale, previous appraisals, and relevant background materials. You will be taking another step toward assuring yourself a fair appraisal.

If you worry that in today's volatile market there's still plenty of room for oversight, confusion, and honest mistakes, you may want to take a few further precautions. You can, for instance, spot-check your appraisal easily and inexpensively. Send a photograph and description of one or two objects to one of the auction galleries that offer free appraisals. If the objects are small, you can take them to the gallery for on-the-spot appraisals. If the auctioneer's staff arrives at a figure close to the one you have on your written appraisal, you can be more certain of its validity. You can also spot-check an appraisal yourself by watching prices at shows, auctions, and in dealer's shops.

For very valuable items, it may pay to have a second independent appraisal. Appraising is far from an exact science. Even the professionals agree that an appraisal is only as good as the appraiser who made it.

Keep appraisals up-to-date. This can be an expensive proposition for those who collect items showing rapid price increases. Only you can decide how much time and money you want to spend on the procedure.

INSURANCE

One of the reasons for having an appraisal is to establish the value of your collection before insuring it. The whole subject of insurance, however, like the appraisal itself, often poses a dilemma for collectors. Should they spend the money to insure their antiques and assure their peace of mind? Or should they gamble that their collection will not fall prey to fire or theft? Once again, the choice is not easy or clear-cut; the answer must be personal, one that suits both the collector and the collection.

It makes no sense, for example, to insure an object that has great sentimental value, but little financial worth. And collectors who find either the paperwork or the constant need for reappraisal onerous will probably choose not to insure. However, if your collection is becoming increasingly valuable—has, in fact, reached the point that you cannot afford to replace what might be damaged or stolen—then perhaps your peace of mind is worth the price of the premium. The money you receive in the settlement of a claim may never assuage the pain of loss you'll feel, but it may prevent financial disaster and allow you to purchase something else you love.

Buying insurance is like buying any other more tangible product. It pays to study the subject and to shop around.

Start by examining your homeowner's policy. The standard provisions insure the dwelling for a certain amount and the contents for fifty percent of that figure. Thus, if your house were insured for $100,000, you would have $50,000 coverage on the contents. If you rent, a tenant homeowner's policy will cover only the contents of your home.

This may be all the coverage you'll need if your collection is not yet very valuable. Remember, however, that if you have a collection worth, say, $10,000, or even one valuable piece, such as an eighteenth-century secretary or a painting, you'll have that much less coverage on your other furnishings in case of a major loss. A homeowner's policy covers all the items in your home—from fine furniture to toothbrushes.

Standard homeowner's policies vary. You may have the basic form, which provides minimum coverage; the broad form, which insures you against a greater number of perils; or what is called an "all risk" policy. But, in fact, very few homeowner's policies are "all risk," because a list of exclusions generally follows the list of "perils insured against."

Most of the policies have a deductible of $50 or $100, which you must pay yourself before you can begin to recover a loss. And there are often "limits of liability" in which the company refuses to pay more than a fixed amount for all losses in a category, such as silver or jewelry, in any one occurrence.

Another difficulty that can arise with homeowner's coverage stems from the fact that all the items are *unscheduled,* that is, unlisted. It is up to the owners to prove what they had and how much it was worth at the time of the loss. No easy task. If you decide that your antiques and collectibles are sufficiently covered by your homeowner's policy, it is imperative that you keep very good records, including receipts and appraisals. Take photographs of everything; make sure that your inventory list includes complete descriptions as well as current values (see pp. 75–79).

Should you decide that your coverage is not enough, you will want to look into a personal articles floater policy.

Floater policies can be written as supplements to a homeowner's policy or as separate documents. They cover a variety of categories such as jewelry, furs, or fine arts, which owners find too valuable—and insurance companies too risky—for standard coverage. The fine arts category includes antiques and collectibles as well as paintings and sculpture. It may not include coins or stamps.

Floater policies have several advantages. The most important, probably, is that each item is scheduled or listed, and given a value. Should a loss occur, you do not have to prove anything; the insurers accept the fact that you owned the item, that it was stolen or damaged, and they will settle the claim. They will not, however, always pay the full amount for which the item was insured. You may receive less. This is one reason it pays to investigate several companies before you buy a policy.

Floaters are more truly "all risk" than homeowner's policies. You are covered, for example, for "mysterious disappearance"—an incident that cannot be proven a theft and may even be due to your own negligence.

But even they do not provide *total* coverage. In most fine arts floater policies you are not insured for damages resulting from repairing, restoring, or retouching, or for the breakage of fragile objects. You can, however, buy additional coverage for breakage and, depending on what you collect, how valuable it is, and how frequently you move it or touch it, that may be worth the extra expense.

Most floater policies do not contain a deductible clause.

What are the disadvantages? The additional cost can, of course, be a factor. Also, some insurance companies require professional appraisals when you take out the policy and at specified intervals thereafter. (If you're insuring an object you've recently bought, you may be able to submit a bill of sale as evidence of value.) Many collectors find these frequent appraisals annoying and expensive; they consider them to be the major disadvantage to the fine arts policy. And if you collect objects that are appreciating rapidly, it can be a problem.

The Chubb Group of Insurance Companies, which probably carries more fine arts policies than any other company, does not require a professional appraisal unless an item is highly unusual. You'll still have to follow the market, yourself, however, to know when to revalue your collection and increase your coverage.

Chubb also issues what is called an "insured for–valued at" policy. That means that in case of loss you will receive the full amount of the policy. Many other companies reserve the right to pay less—whatever figure they deem the object to be "valued at," no matter what its insured value is.

If you think that the advantages of a floater policy may outweigh the disadvantages, investigate further. Check first with the agent who handles your homeowner's policy. Insurance advisors agree that it is more efficient if you can keep your homeowner's and floater policies with the same company. A settlement can be made more easily and more quickly.

However, you should also check with other agents, especially if your collection is very valuable. The cost of the premiums can vary from one company to another. So can some important provisions, such as the insured for–valued at clause described above.

Here are a few areas to examine with an agent.

1. *Exclusions.* Find out exactly what is covered and what is not. Ask questions if you don't understand the terminology.

2. *Off-premises coverage.* Are your antiques insured while they're on loan to a museum or at a repair shop?

3. *Pairs and sets.* If one piece of a pair or a set is damaged or stolen the insurers will reimburse you for the full value of the pair or set, but you must surrender to them any remaining pieces in the set. Be sure you understand this provision. If you don't like the terms, ask if any options are available.

4. *New purchases.* Many policies will cover any new objects you buy after the policy is written provided you notify the company within a specified period of time after purchase and then pay the additional premium. Such purchases usually cannot exceed twenty-five percent of the total amount of insurance.

Always ask to see the complete policy before you agree to its coverage. The written policy—not what the agent said or what you think he said—determines the coverage. Although some companies have made progress in translating their unintelligible language into plain English, you will still have to read the fine print carefully.

Losing a collection to fire or theft is tragedy enough; make sure no further unpleasant surprises await you when you file your claim.

PROTECTING AGAINST THEFT

The statistics can be frightening: 2,017,922 residential burglaries were committed in the United States during 1978. More than 10,000 pieces of fine art are stolen in a single year.

But law enforcement officials stress that the facts are not meant to create panic. A thief, they say, is an opportunist, a criminal who will select the easiest target. Make it difficult for him to enter your home and he's likely to move on to another place where the work is easier and the risk of being caught is less.

Your best protection lies in your own attitude, in doing what you can to keep your home secure. You need not be so fearful that you lie awake at night or will not take a vacation; neither should you be so nonchalant that you take no precautions and expect the police to take care of you and your collection.

The FBI, which keeps nationwide records on all crime, reports a few other facts that you should know. First, one-fifth of all burglaries are classified "unlawful entry without force." That means the thief did not have to break a window, jimmy a lock, or smash a door to get in. He simply walked or climbed in.

Second, in 1978 persons under twenty-five accounted for eighty-four percent of all arrests for burglary. Fifty-two percent were under eighteen.

Third, daytime residential burglaries are on the increase. Thieves prefer their targets to be unoccupied, and houses are more likely to be empty during the day. In addition, in many states the sentence is harsher for thieves who steal at night than for those who commit a daytime crime.

These facts should help you prepare your line of defense. Even before you look into sturdy locks and other security systems, examine your house as it might appear to a criminal.

Does it ever look unoccupied? Don't leave the garage door open if it reveals an empty space. If you are going on vacation, stop deliveries of mail, milk, and newspapers. Ask a neighbor to watch for—and remove—unexpected packages. Have the snow shoveled, the grass cut, and the leaves raked. You can also ask the neighbors to park their car in front of your house or in your driveway occasionally. Use automatic timers to turn lights and radios on and off at likely times. Police recommend at least two—one in the living room or kitchen and one in a bedroom.

Never leave a key under the mat, in a mailbox, or on a ledge. Thieves know every likely hiding place. Don't leave notes that reveal your plans: "Back in an hour." You're asking for a burglary if you allow the local newspaper to announce a vacation or a business trip. Thieves are callous enough to read the obituary pages, note the time of a funeral, and break into the home while the family is at the cemetery.

Keep your shrubbery trimmed away from windows and doors, especially those entries that are secluded. Use entrance lamps and outdoor spotlights. But, police caution, lights left burning during the day are a sure sign of an empty house.

Thieves hate lights, noise, and anything else that draws attention to their activities. They also hate to encounter their victims. If you make use of these facts in planning your own protection, you should be able to discourage a thief from even approaching your door.

Your main line of defense, however, should be sturdy locks on all vulnerable doors and windows.

Walk through your house and note all entrances that might provide access for a thief. Don't overlook garage windows and doors, sliding glass doors that lead to a patio, basement windows and doors. Law enforcement officials report that second-story burglaries are not so common these days, so concentrate on first-floor windows and doors, particularly those in secluded places on the side or in the back of your house.

In many towns the police department, as a public service, will send a member of the force to your home to point out its vulnerable areas and make specific suggestions for the proper security measures. You can also get some pointers from a good locksmith. His recommendations will vary, depending on your house or apartment, the doors, and the existing locks you have. He may suggest, for example, dual-cylinder locks for doors with glass panes. Dual cylinders require a key to be opened from the inside as well as from the outside. Even if a thief breaks the glass, he cannot get into the house without a key.

The sturdiest lock, the kind the police recommend, is the dead-bolt lock. Segal maintains its reputation for the best such lock, but other manufacturers also produce satisfactory varieties. Locks that carry the UL (Underwriters Laboratory) label have been carefully tested and offer excellent security. Unless you're very proficient at woodworking, you should have a professional install your locks.

Some collectors are already aware of the additional protection the new electronic burglar-alarm systems can provide. These wireless devices, which operate on battery-powered transmitters, are called *perimeter alarm systems* because they alert you—or the neighbors or the police—that a burglar is trying to enter your house. (*Space* systems, however, sound an alarm only after someone is inside your house.)

In the typical wireless system sensors are placed on windows and doors. When activated, these sensors send a signal to a central control unit, which then sets off the alarm. The console usually works on regular house current, but can also be battery-powered. The systems are sold in kits, with a combination of door sensors and window sensors plus the central console. You can add components to the basic kit as you wish. Options include extra door and window sensors, smoke detectors, remote sirens that can be mounted outside your home, automatic telephone alerts to the local police and fire departments.

These wireless systems are not inexpensive. However, you can do the installation yourself and save on the high labor costs usually associated with alarm systems.

Be sure you know what you're buying. Deal only with reputable companies. Your local police may be able to give you the name of a respected firm in the area. If you're looking at name brands, comparison shop. Prices vary. But don't make your decision solely on the basis of price. Each brand offers different components in the basic kit, and there may be other less obvious differences, too.

Assume the unlikely: that a thief is not fooled by your automatic timers or intimidated by your spotlights, that he finds an unlocked window with no sensor and gains access to your house.

There are still several ways to thwart him and protect your collection. You can, of course, keep everything hidden. One eccentric collector constructed an elaborate system of rods and pulleys so he could hang an old tapestry on the wall of his bedroom. To the uninitiated it looked like an ordinary, if cumbersome, decoration. Those with whom he shared his secret knew the tapestry covered recessed floor-to-ceiling shelves that contained his valuable collection of early American clocks. One could wonder if he had not sacrificed enjoyment to security. There are less extreme ways to protect a collection. You can place certain very valuable objects in locked cases. Or you can mark the objects with your name, social security number, or any other code number you choose. Marked objects are more difficult for a thief to pass along and, therefore, easier for the police to retrieve and identify.

Operation Identification, a crime-prevention program sponsored by many police departments, is based on marked items. You, or the police, engrave a code number on your valuable objects; the number is kept on file with the police. Operation Identification stickers on your doors and windows warn thieves that the objects they steal may very well prove useless to them.

There are actually several ways to mark your antiques and collectibles. An invisible ink, which can only be seen under black light, can be used to mark cloth, ceramic, or paper objects. A similar ink has been designed specifically for metal objects. Tungsten carbide or diamond engraving tools etch identifying numbers in glass, stone, plastic, wood, and many other surfaces.

Take care when you mark the objects. Read the instructions carefully; use the proper tool for each substance. And, finally, consider whether marking your antiques or collectibles will make them less marketable if you should ever decide to sell them.

A few final precautions:

1. If you lend your collection to a library or museum, *request an anonymous credit line.* Be sure that the institution has taken sufficient security measures to protect your collection and that it has enough insurance to cover all the objects.
2. If you allow your collection to be photographed for a magazine article or a book, *do not permit your name and address to appear in print.*
3. If you advertise to buy or sell, *use a box number* rather than your street address in the ad.

PROTECTING AGAINST FIRE

Start with the basics. Many fires can be traced to faulty heating systems, improper wiring, or clogged chimneys. Check these trouble spots regularly. Other fires happen because people ignore elementary safety rules. *Don't.*

If a fire does break out, especially at night when everyone is asleep, fire detectors provide an essential early warning and thus protect you. Detectors are generally divided into two types. The ionization detector responds to an invisible amount of combustion particles in the air and sounds an alarm in the earliest stage of the fire. The photoelectric detector, also called a smoke detector, responds to combustion particles that have become dense enough to be visible as smoke. Either variety provides sufficient warning to allow you to escape and also call for help. Some of the newest models combine both techniques.

Detectors are usually battery-operated and are now inexpensive enough so that you can install one on each floor, or near each sleeping area of your home. Some of the electronic burglar-alarm systems (see p. 89) can be set up to include smoke detectors.

After you've installed fire detectors, you should also invest in a portable fire extinguisher. Residential extinguishers are labeled A, B, and C, depending on the kind of fire to be extinguished. Fires in paper, wood, or fabric require A; flammable liquids, such as fuel, oil, gasoline, grease, or solvents, require B; electrical fires, C. A multipurpose extinguisher labeled ABC will put out most types of fires.

Collectors have an additional problem. They must put out the fire quickly and thoroughly. But they would prefer not to damage their valuable collection in the process. Extinguishers that are water-based or that contain chemicals can ruin art or antiques. One type of extinguisher that puts out A, B, and C fires and does not harm a collection is Halon 1301, produced by the du Pont Co.

Halon 1301 is also available in sprinkler systems. Because the sprinklers emit gases, instead of water, the system does no damage. Few collectors, however, will find such a total system necessary for their homes.

DISPOSING OF A COLLECTION

Many collectors cannot bear to think of selling, especially when they are buying. We buy because we love a piece, because it will fill a spot in our collection, our living room, our heart.

Nevertheless, the time often comes when you should sell. It may be wise for financial reasons. You may want to trade-up or rid your collection of some mistakes. You may have lost your interest in, say, spongeware and found a new specialty: Western art.

These are all valid, and quite common, reasons for selling. Don't hesitate. Or, rather, hesitate only long enough to determine the most efficient and most profitable way to sell. Selling antiques and collectibles, whether you intend to part with an entire collection or only a few selected items, can be more difficult than buying them. It will be to your definite advantage to think the matter through and select your procedure carefully.

Your first step should be to determine what you want to sell. That sounds obvious; but it bears closer examination. When you're selling an entire collection, your approach will be quite different from when you are selling only one or two items. Don't be tempted to sell only the good pieces in your collection. You'll lessen the value of the remaining

pieces. It's better to try first to arrange a package deal. If you have collected items of regional interest—Long Island stoneware, for example—
and must sell some things because you're moving to the Midwest, remember that, despite the extensive traveling dealers and collectors do,
regional items still tend to bring higher prices in the area in which they
were made.

You may also want to consider the length of time you've owned the
objects. On good pieces that you've had for a long time, you'll no doubt
get your money back and probably even make a fair profit. Generally,
experts agree, it takes approximately seven years for the wholesale prices
at which you must sell to reach the retail level at which you probably
bought. So if you are choosing among several items to sell—all other
things being equal—sell the pieces you've owned the longest. (This advice assumes that you have some room to maneuver, to make choices
between objects. If for some reason there is no choice, then your decision has been made for you.)

After you know what you want to sell, gather all the information you
have on the objects—photographs, original bills, appraisals, correspondence, notes on repairs, and so forth (see pp. 75–79). As you review the
material, think about two things: What makes your object(s) marketable? And to whom?

A collector who has put together a fascinating, wide-ranging display
on the history of magic may be able to sell the entire collection to another individual with similar interests. If not, he may have to approach
toy collectors, rare book collectors, poster/print collectors, and auto-
graph collectors in order to find a receptive market. The same is true of
other collections that cross the boundaries into a variety of specialties. A
collector of racing toys—dog racing, horseracing, car racing—had difficulty selling that collection as an entity. He had no trouble at all when
he decided to break up the grouping and sell individual items to mechanical bank collectors, sports historians and race track enthusiasts,
among others.

So think creatively. Would any of your items, or the entire collection,
fit into one of the many specialized auctions now held in the large regional galleries? Would they be of interest to a particular corporation?
Could a decorator use them for her clients?

Once you have a general idea of who might buy your antiques, and
why, you can begin to examine the specific avenues for selling: auctions,

dealers, flea markets, tag sales, advertisements, and so forth. You may prefer to sell by the same methods you use to buy. Collectors who frequent auction galleries often sell through them, too. Those who buy from dealers usually offer a collection to them first. Before you make a final decision, consider all the options.

Each of the avenues is examined in detail in the following pages. But there are a few general guidelines that will apply to any path you choose.

1. *Know the retail value of what you're selling.* Check out the market before you settle on a price at which you'll sell. Use dealer prices at shows or flea markets, price guides, appraisals—whatever gives you an idea of current market values.

2. *Do not expect to get the current market price when you sell,* even if you sell to another private individual.

3. *Allow yourself as much time as possible.* Remember that antiques and collectibles were never meant to be as liquid as stocks. There are ways to get money quickly if you must, but don't let haste push you into a deal you'll regret.

4. *Adopt a sales mentality.* Be confident; be optimistic. Don't apologize for selling, whatever your reason. Whether you're approaching a dealer, an auctioneer, or another collector, assume they'll want what you're offering. If they do, you're in luck. If they don't, someone else surely will. After all, you once did.

AUCTIONS

Auction galleries are busy places these days, and that can be good news for a collector who has something to sell. Auctioneers are actively, sometimes fiercely, competing for consignments. One woman who inquired about auctioning some of her Victorian furniture was surprised and flattered to find herself pursued by long-distance telephone calls.

The rapid spread of the buyer's premium (see p. 48), which requires that the seller pay only a ten-percent commission instead of the more usual twenty or twenty-five percent, attests to the willingness of more and more houses to accommodate the seller. Christie's initiated the ten-and-ten system in the United States in 1977, and many New York galleries were soon forced to follow. The system then spread to other regional houses, among them, Skinner in Massachusetts, and Sloan and

Weschler in Washington, D.C., who found they could not compete for high-quality consignments if they did not offer the new rate structure. Although a few regional galleries and many of the lower-ranked houses do not offer such an attractive rate, the auction market is, in general, a seller's market these days. It doesn't matter whether you have a few items to sell, an entire collection, or a houseful of furniture and accessories. You should at the very least thoroughly investigate this method before making your decision.

Auction galleries can attract a large group of interested buyers. The most prestigious advertise nationally and have extensive mailing lists. Even the smaller galleries advertise in local papers and trade publications. If your objects fit into a specialized sale—Americana or Victoriana, or Orientalia; bottles, toys, or art pottery—you're fortunate. Specialty auctions can bring prices fifteen to twenty percent higher than a more general auction. You profit from the competition among interested buyers.

Among the disadvantages of selling by auction are, first, the hidden costs: the items you will find on your bill that are not included in the ten percent—or even a twenty-five percent—commission. At most auction houses, for instance, you must pay transportation and insurance costs. You may also have to pick up the charges for advertising or for photographs to be used in a catalogue.

A second disadvantage is the comparatively long time between the day you consign the items and the day of the auction and then between the sale and the receipt of payment. A few houses will pay within ten days but many contracts give the auctioneer thirty-five days to settle your account. The wait may, in fact, be even longer. If you need cash quickly, selling by auction is not the route to follow. (Some auction houses do buy outright, but you should check with a few dealers before you sell to an auction gallery. You may be able to do better with the dealers.)

The third—and perhaps most important—disadvantage is the risk factor. While the appeal of an auction is that good things can happen for a seller as well as for a buyer, many collectors are not willing to gamble. There are, they believe, too many unknowns and they prefer the safety of a sale in which prices cannot change after they sign on the dotted line.

As you look further into auctions, keep in mind the objects you're selling and the potential buyers. The objective is to put your consignments before the largest—and most likely—group of bidders. Don't dismiss the top international galleries. They handle a variety of objects and these days they will accept items worth "in the hundreds"—even less if they are part of a large consignment. The regional houses accept an even broader range of antiques and collectibles. By reading the ads in the trade publications, you will pick up some clues to which houses seem to specialize in which categories. The country auctioneers will take anything, but you cannot expect to draw large crowds or high prices. Keep in mind also that you will want to deal with a reputable organization and that you will make a larger profit if you keep your costs down.

HOW TO PROCEED

Contact a number of auctioneers and tell them what you have to sell. Depending on distance, the size of the consignment, house policy, and so forth, they will then suggest a procedure: you send photographs and descriptions of the items, or, if they are easily carried, bring them to the gallery, or someone from the gallery will visit your home to inspect the items. Local auctioneers are most likely to come to your home. But the top houses will, too, if you're selling a large quantity of high-quality items. Always ask if there is a charge for this service. Once the auctioneer or his representative has seen what you have to sell, he will give you a rough estimate of what he thinks it will bring at auction.

It will then be time to ask some further questions. Here is a checklist of the points you should cover in any preliminary discussion.

1. *What is the commission?* Is it a flat rate? Or a sliding scale—twenty percent on items over $500, say, twenty-five percent on items under $500?
2. *What other costs will you incur?* Shipping? Insurance? Advertising? Photographs for a catalogue?
3. *Are reserves allowed?* How are they determined? What is the fee if the house must buy-in a lot for you?
4. *When will the sale be held?* What kind of sale will it be? Specialized? Catalogue?
5. *What kind of advertising will precede the sale?*
6. *When will payment be made?*
7. *What is the procedure if some of your consignments do not sell?*
8. *Ask to see a sample contract.* Study it carefully.

Certain elements may be more important to you than others. Will your objects really benefit from national advertising? Do you want your money in ten days, or thirty-five? Are trucking charges to a distant gallery prohibitively expensive? Are you willing to allow your collection to be sold without reserve?

The reserve is your protection against an extremely low bid that could be the result of poor attendance, bad weather, or the maneuvering of a dealers' ring. Some auctioneers do not allow consignors to use any reserve. Others will accept a reserve at a rate they specify, usually at or below the low of their presale estimate.

Often the reserve is a fixed percentage of the presale estimate. C. G. Sloan in Washington, D.C., for instance, sets the reserve at forty percent of the low presale estimate. Policies vary from house to house, so if the amount of the reserve is important to you, make that figure the basis for choosing one gallery instead of another.

Idealists may wish that the auction market could float free without any encumbrances to inflate prices, but at the present time it is unwise for most private individuals to sell at auction without utilizing the reserve. However, if your purpose is to sell an object, then placing too high a reserve can only interfere with that objective. This is why it pays to know market values.

If you are offering a particularly large or very fine consignment, you may want to ask for a few other concessions from the auctioneer. Some houses, for example, will negotiate a lower commission rate on exceptional items, especially if they want to keep you from going to another gallery. Some auctioneers will agree to place your lot in prime selling time (not at the beginning or the end of the auction) and in a good location during the presale exhibition. You will probably only accomplish these ploys if you have leverage: a desirable consignment, the promise of future consignments, or a long and faithful relationship. You are a private individual dealing with a large and complex market; you'll do best by looking out for your own interests.

DEALERS

Because dealers sell the majority of antiques and collectibles in this country, they are an excellent market when you want to sell. They must buy. And they do—from auction galleries, other dealers, private collectors, you.

The key lies in finding the dealer who wants what you have to sell and who will pay your asking price. Once again keep in mind the objects you want to sell. If you have fine furniture, you may want to start with a dealer who belongs to the rather exclusive National Antique and Art Dealers Association of America, Inc., headquartered at 59 East 57th Street, New York, N.Y. 10022. Or you can visit one of the large charity shows and look for a dealer who sells items of a quality and period similar to yours. The antiques supermarkets offer another efficient way to locate a compatible dealer. Many collectors who only occasionally sell an item carry it with them to shows or supermarkets and peddle it while they shop for new items.

If you are selling items from a specific category, Victorian jewelry or carnival glass, for example, contact dealers who specialize in that area. Don't be limited to those in your own city or town; write to any others about whom you've heard or read. Dealers travel.

This approach also gives you an opportunity to choose between an outright sale and a trade. A dealer, particularly one from whom you may have bought the piece originally, is often willing to allow you more on a trade-in than she would on a sale. For example, you want to get rid of a Weller vase. Your price is $55.00. A dealer may offer you $40.00 cash or $55.00 toward the purchase of another, more expensive Weller piece.

Whichever dealer you approach, be sure you know his or her reputation. Select one who is known for integrity—and who also has a good credit rating. Avoid *pickers*. These are the people who scout for dealers. They often advertise in the Yellow Pages under headings such as "We Buy Anything." They do, but at the lowest possible prices. They must keep buying and selling; they usually care little for quality and are interested primarily in a fast sale. Be particularly wary of pickers if you have a house full of things to sell. They can skim off the best, that is, the most marketable, pieces and leave you with the less desirable items.

Once you have decided on an appropriate dealer, there are three possible ways to negotiate the sale. The trade-in, described above, usually involves no cash. Essentially you replace an object you no longer want with one you do and, with luck, accomplish the transaction with some financial gain, even if it is not immediately apparent in dollars and cents.

A second way to sell is on consignment. You allow a dealer to keep your Windsor chairs in her shop in the hope that she can sell them more easily than you can. Because she is not actually buying them from you, she doesn't pay you until a customer pays her. And because she is not laying out her own money for the chairs, her fee is lower (usually between fifteen percent and thirty percent of the final sale price) than if she bought them outright.

The risks of selling on consignment are that the chairs may not sell for some time (or at all), that they may be damaged while on display, that the dealer will perhaps not try very hard to sell furniture she does not own or report honestly the final sale price.

You can minimize these risks by working out a written agreement with the dealer before you leave the chairs in her shop. Be sure that any agreement includes the following points:

1. *Detailed description of all items*—including any imperfections, repairs, and so forth.
2. *Sale price*—to be marked on items—and the *dealer's commission*.
3. *Responsibility for transportation, loss, damage,* and so forth.
4. *Repairs.* If the dealer recommends them, be sure you know exactly what she plans to do and how much more than her stated commission she'll charge.
5. *Length of time objects will be on consignment.* Three to six months is probably reasonable in today's market.
6. *Date of payment.* How long after the date of sale will you receive your money? In cash? Check?

Be sure the agreement is dated and signed by both parties. You should keep a copy; the dealer keeps another. If you are selling very valuable items, you may want to have the agreement notarized to assure yourself of greater legal protection. Check, too, that your insurance—or the dealer's—provides adequate coverage.

The third—and by far the most common—way of selling to dealers is the outright cash-on-the-line sale. This is, in fact, the primary attraction of placing an object with a dealer. Most of them are prepared to open their cash drawer or checkbook and pay you immediately.

The difficulty, at least for sellers, is that dealers seldom pay more than fifty to seventy-five percent of an item's retail value. (On less-than-quality objects the percentage may go even lower.) They must allow enough to cover their own expenses plus their markup.

Your objective should be to get the best price you can. Don't be afraid to talk to several different dealers. The one time this procedure can backfire is when you have an exceedingly rare or valuable piece to sell. Dealers talk; if you approach too many, the word will quickly spread that the piece is "hot," and you may then find it difficult to sell anywhere. This is, however, a special situation. In most cases it will pay to comparison shop and to bargain.

Dealers will seldom suggest the price at which they'll buy. You can try to maneuver them into such a situation, but almost always they prefer the seller to name a price. Negotiations begin there. If the dealer is interested, he'll come back with his own offer, which is usually much lower. You can handle this situation by making your opening price somewhat higher than the figure you'll ultimately accept. It is, quite simply, the reverse of buying where you start at a lower figure than you're prepared to pay and work upward. Here you'll be moving downward. If you know the retail value of what you're selling, you'll know when an offer seems fair. In any case remember that a dealer will start bargaining far below the level he can actually afford.

You can improve your chances of selling well by selecting the dealers who can resell your objects quickly; by approaching them at opportune moments, before a large show, for example, and by offering them quality objects that have not been on the market recently.

Two final messages—both urging caution—are necessary. First, do not be rushed or intimidated by disparaging comments, or duped by variations on old con games. Not all dealers are honest; some try to come by their stock as cheaply as possible, even if they must stretch the truth to do it. Know what you're selling; don't be talked into selling something else or into settling for a lower price because the item is alleged to be "damaged" or "inferior."

Second, insist on cash or investigate the credit rating of a dealer whom you don't know before you give him the object. When you buy, you must very often pay cash or establish your credit. It is only common sense to expect the same when someone you don't know buys from you.

ON BECOMING A DEALER

As most collectors eventually learn, there is a very thin line between being a collector and a dealer. The change is really more of an expansion than a transformation. Collectors and dealers inhabit the same world—auctions, shows, shops, flea markets, clubs—and read the same magazines and newspapers. At some point a collector begins to trust his own judgment so surely that he wants to buy for others. Or he decides to buy for resale so he can afford to continue collecting. Or he buys to sell because he can't resist a bargain—any bargain. Whatever the reasons, many collectors slide over the line and become professionals. Some, determined to pursue a full-time career, use their capital to open a shop. Others operate from home on a "by appointment" basis or travel the show circuit on weekends. Doing a show involves hours of packing and unpacking, but it also allows the dealers to buy before the show actually begins—a privilege many collectors find worth the work. Still others sell only by mail. You can pursue any of these options depending on the amount of time and money you're prepared to invest.

Turning professional is not a step to be taken lightly. You will need to know about inventory procedures, sales-tax numbers, balance sheets, and so forth—all topics beyond the scope of this book. But all collectors have a stake in the dealers of the future. If you have enjoyed collecting, then perhaps you owe your future customers no less than your best effort. And becoming an honest, knowledgeable dealer, in any area, is hard work.

FLEA MARKETS

One way to straddle the fence—to remain a collector but become a once-in-a-while dealer—is to sell occasionally at a small antiques show or flea market. One collector who regularly changes his specialties just as regularly cleans out his unwanted collectibles at flea markets. "It's found money," he says. And if you enjoy a day of meeting people, bargaining with them, and selling without pressure, it is found pleasure, too.

Some flea markets are better than others. You already know which ones are best for buying what interests you. When you're thinking of setting up to sell, you must look at the markets from a different perspective. Some attract only browsers; others cater to special-interest groups. Before you decide to join a market, visit it several times at peak hours. Look at the other dealers' merchandise. Is it similar in quality to your own? Look at the customers. How many are there? Are they buying? Ask questions. Does the market have a good reputation? Is it accessible, well publicized, well run?

When you decide on a market you'd like to try, visit the promoter. He'll tell you what he provides, and what you pay. Many promoters now require a deposit in advance; this reserves your place. At some markets you may be able to arrive the day of the sale and simply set up, but don't expect that at a popular market during busy weekends.

Before you sign a contract, if one is required, find out the size of the space you'll be allotted and where it will be. Ask for a good location, preferably near dealers of similar objects. Will tables be provided? They occasionally are at outdoor markets; if not you bring your own or use the tailgate of your station wagon. If you are looking into an outdoor market, try to choose one with a rain date. This is particularly important if you sell only once or twice a year or if the flea market is not open every weekend.

Set up your display so that objects are visible and protected. Be sure you can keep an eye on everything from where you sit or stand. Put small objects on tables or in shallow, lightweight display cases. Price objects at what you consider to be a fair price but expect bargaining and allow yourself enough room to come down. Most customers at a flea market object to paying "full" price.

Bring plenty of old newspapers, paper bags, and shopping bags with you. Also be prepared to make change; have small bills and coins handy, but out of sight.

Flea markets can be an ideal way to dispose of a variety of items that are inappropriate for auctions or dealers. But beware. The market seduces. You may wind up buying more than you sell.

TAG SALES

These events, so attractive to buyers and sellers, run the gamut from one-day mini-sales to the three-day professionally run, everything-must-go extravaganzas.

The kind and number of items you want to sell will probably determine the kind of sale you'll have. If you are redecorating or cleaning out some early mistakes and can put together a good selection of items, run the sale yourself. It will take organization, time, and effort, but the profits will be all yours.

Before you do anything else, check the local ordinances. Will you need a license? Are there parking regulations you must observe? Can you advertise? The next step is to set a date. Weekends during the spring, summer, and fall are best. If you're planning only a one-day sale, try Saturday; for a three-day sale, Friday, Saturday, and Sunday. There are advantages to three-day sales. Although there is more work for you and you should have more objects to sell, your fixed expenses, such as advertising, will remain the same. You allow time for the news to spread by word of mouth and you can hope to sell more by marking everything down on the last day. You also protect yourself in case of bad weather.

Once you've chosen a date, plan your advertising strategy. Use every free resource your community offers. Put posters or notices on bulletin boards in libraries, supermarkets, churches, schools, and railroad and bus stations. Tell your friends, neighbors, and co-workers. The day of the sale, if no local laws prohibit such notices, put large, clearly printed signs—with directions—on the telephone poles and street markers near your home.

Compose an ad for the classified column of your local newspaper. Most papers have special headings for "garage sales" or "house sales." Choose the items or categories you think will be big sellers and put them in the ad. Then say "much, much more" or "other things too numerous to mention." Give the date and time. You can add "No Early Birds," but this probably won't work. Include your address, of course, and directions, if you think they're necessary. Leave your phone number out if you want to keep your sanity—and your good humor.

Advertising may be the key to attracting customers. But the way to please them is to have your merchandise fairly priced and well displayed. Selling at tag sales is really no different from selling at auctions, through dealers, or at flea markets; you'll do best when you know the current market prices for what you have to sell. Do your homework at flea markets and other tag sales. You can check the price guides, but they may not be accurate for your area. Then put tags on everything. Write clearly—in ink. And keep a separate price list of your own in case the tags are lost or misplaced.

When you set up the sale, try to think out traffic patterns. How will people enter? Where will they go first? Give them room to move around and see things without breaking anything. Put up signs: "Watch Your Step," "Stairs," "No Smoking." Arrange small items in cases or on tables. Plan on a single exit—and station yourself there with a cashbox or drawer. If your family or friends are willing to help, ask them to keep an eye on both the antiques and the customers.

Many people, especially collectors, may have to dispose of a houseful of furniture and accessories. These are the times when it may be wise to rely on professional liquidators or tag sale operators. Although you can run such a house sale yourself, the work involved can be staggering. Then, too, few people are knowledgeable enough in all areas to price competitively.

The tag sale operators usually are. They will first look through the house and give you an estimate of what the sale will probably bring. Some operators will not accept a sale that will gross less than $3000 or $4000. For their work and their expertise you pay them a commission, usually twenty-five percent of the total sale.

Once you agree to the sale, they will take over all the details. They will check out local ordinances; they'll place the ad in the newspaper (although you may have to pay for it). Their staff will spend the days before the sale going through closets and drawers, organizing, pricing, displaying everything. On the days of the sale they will provide security, if necessary, as well as enough helpers to answer questions, direct traffic, and handle the money. At the end of the sale you should get an itemized inventory list. Everything should be numbered with the price asked and the price received noted.

Before you agree to let a tag sale operator handle your things, check out all these points with her. If possible, attend one of her sales. Word-of-mouth recommendations are valuable; ask around. Find out what buyers—and sellers—think of her sales. Once you've found a reliable, trustworthy person, relax and let her do the work. She may underprice some items, but on the whole, she'll probably do better for you than you could do yourself.

SELLING BY MAIL

Selling your antiques or collectibles by mail can be as simple as answering a "Wanted to Buy" ad in one of the trade publications. Or it could turn into a major sales campaign involving sophisticated market analysis and direct-mail techniques as well as advertising. Once again your clues come from the number and kind of items you're selling. Your objective is to sell them with a minimum of time, effort, and expense. So, first check the "Wanted to Buy" ads; you may not even have to run an ad of your own. There is a difference between the sweeping "We Buy Anything" ads that pickers place and those run by more selective buyers. Dealers and private collectors routinely place ads under various specialty headings, for example, guns, bottles, dolls. Other collectibles often appear in the "miscellaneous wanted" classifieds. Read all the ads carefully. Decide which one, or ones, you will answer. Unless the ad specifically invites you to send merchandise, write first. Describe what you have clearly and honestly. If the advertiser is interested, he will write back. You will then have to set your price or respond to his, if he makes an offer

If you do not find any appropriate ads, try placing one of your own. Most of the antiques and collectibles periodicals charge reasonable rates for classified ads. If you think your sale will be worth the expense, run a display ad with a decorative border or photograph. You may have to experiment, too. If one large ad doesn't bring any buyers, try a smaller ad that runs in several issues. Compose an ad that is both brief and clear. Describe what you have—a collection, a single object, a mixture. You may want to include a price; or you may prefer to wait until the answers come in.

In either case you will have to face up to the central issue—pricing—sooner or later. Once again, know the market value for each object you're selling. If you're looking for a quick sale, price slightly under competitive prices in other ads or at shows. Dealers will seldom make an offer; you must state what your asking price is. This procedure can create problems for collectors who sell by mail. They fear that if their first price is too high, the dealer may not respond and they will have lost the opportunity to bargain. It *is* easier to keep negotiations fluid in person. But if you can entice several prospective buyers to answer your ad, and you price fairly, chances are not all of them will find your price a stumbling block.

If you're selling many individual items—too many to include in an ad—you can prepare and advertise a list. Offer the list free; you can request a self-addressed stamped envelope if you must keep costs to a minimum. When you prepare your list, be specific on sizes and markings. Include any references to standard texts, if possible, and your asking price. Be clear on instructions. "All items mailed parcel post; insurance extra." Make sure you have the proper wrapping materials—many are advertised in the trade papers—and that you are familiar with postal regulations.

Another way to sell a collection is to prepare a carefully worded letter offering the collection, or items from it, to a limited number of interested buyers. This is the most exclusive form of direct-mail advertising and can be very effective for quality items. If you have access to a broader mailing list and want to reach greater numbers of prospective buyers, try a mimeographed or printed flyer. Once again, include all relevant information.

A variation of this direct-mail operation is the mail auction. A collector who feels sure that several other collectors will be interested in bidding for his objects solicits bids by mail and then informs the highest bidder that he is successful. The deal is then completed.

TAX LAWS

Collectors seldom think about taxes until they begin to sell some of their antiques or collectibles. Then several questions arise. May I claim a loss if I must sell at a price below what I paid? May I deduct my expenses? Must I declare a profit?

The answers to these questions depend on whether you consider yourself a collector, an investor, or a dealer—and on whether the IRS agrees with your choice.

If you acquire objects primarily to enjoy them and only occasionally sell them, you remain a collector in the eyes of the IRS. If you buy primarily for the purpose of reselling at a profit, then you are an investor. But the law says you must prove your willingness to sell and it allows you only limited use of and pleasure from the objects. If you consider buying and selling antiques or collectibles your business, even a part-time one, then you are a dealer.

Investors and dealers may take a deduction if they must sell at a loss; collectors may not. Whatever your status, you may deduct certain expenses connected with the object. Investors and dealers write off their expenses in the year in which they were incurred; collectors may only deduct them when the object is sold.

The law reads that both collector and investor should consider any profit on a sale of capital assets—including household furnishings—as a capital gain provided the object has been held a year or longer. A dealer must declare his profits as ordinary income. Dealers who fulfill various state requirements are exempt from paying local sales taxes when they buy, but they are expected to collect and pay sales taxes on what they sell.

There is another way, besides selling, to benefit from the appreciation of value in antiques and collectibles. You can give them away. The IRS allows substantial deductions for donations made to museums, libraries, universities, or other nonprofit institutions. In some cases individuals can legitimately claim as much as thirty percent of their adjusted gross income in such deductions.

The first step is to contact a museum or restoration or library which has or might want objects similar to yours. In the past museums tended to accept everything that was offered to them. They wound up with storerooms filled with objects they couldn't display and often couldn't sell because the donors had expressly forbidden it. Nowadays museums are more selective in what they accept. And unless your collection is so attractive that they'll break their usual pattern, they want gifts with no strings attached. You cannot, in most cases, for example, refuse to allow them the option of selling your collection in order to purchase something else. You cannot demand that they keep it on permanent display or build a special room to house it.

That is not to say that museums don't want gifts. They do. But do some research to find an institution that will welcome and can display, at least some of the time, what you have to give. Don't overlook smaller historic homes and sites that may be operating on a tight budget and would welcome appropriate gifts. Do be sure that the institution you select is recognized as a nonprofit organization by the IRS.

Only you can determine which approach, selling or donating, will be of more financial benefit and which will give you more satisfaction. If you decide that your tax bracket and other variables make it wise for you to give your collection away, you can claim as your deduction the fair market value of the item, or the collection, at the time of the donation. You may need to support your claim with an appraisal, which must be acceptable to the IRS. The safest method is to have a lawyer or tax specialist check the IRS requirements before you make the donation.

Make copies of all relevant records—sales receipts, repair bills, provenance, and so forth. You will want to submit some to the IRS to support your deduction and others to the museum, perhaps, to enhance your gift. Once the gift has been made, be sure to get a receipt from the institution, which you must then submit with your tax return.

If you prefer to give your antiques and collectibles to members of your family, you should look into various ways you can avoid the heavy estate taxes that can be levied on such items after your death. You can, within certain limits, give away objects during your lifetime without paying any gift, inheritance, or income taxes. Check out your options with your lawyer or tax advisor.

The ultimate solution—a dream that many collectors cherish—is to open a museum. The tradition, which has its roots among the earliest collectors in both America and Europe, is not exclusively the province of major collectors such as the Guggenheims or the Rockefellers or the du Ponts. Many small museums around the country are the result of one person's vision and dedication.

◆ In Philadelphia, Pennsylvania, Leon Perelman's exceptional collection of mechanical banks grew to include hundreds of tin and cast-iron toys, as well as dolls. Perelman bought a historic home on Society Hill, not far from Independence Hall, restored it, and opened the Perelman Antique Toy Museum.

◆ In Chattanooga, Tennessee, Anna Safley Houston spent a lifetime collecting a variety of things—mugs, tureens, vases, teapots, paperweights. Her specialty, however, was pitchers and she eventually accumulated 15,000 specimens. Mrs. Houston donated all her collections to a nonprofit organization, which raised funds to buy a home for the collection and now operates the Houston Antique Museum.

◆ In Doylestown, Pennsylvania, the name of Dr. Henry Chapman Mercer summons up one fantastic story after another. At the end of the nineteenth century and the beginning of the twentieth, Dr. Mercer in his somewhat eccentric but very thorough way put together a most impressive collection of Americana, including tools of all the trades plus household and farming implements. Then he personally designed the castlelike structure that houses the Mercer Museum. Mercer intended his collection of more than 30,000 objects to provide visitors with a new view of the history of a nation—and it does.

Not many collectors have the determination to take on such a task. Nor should they. It is enough perhaps to own a bit of the past, to preserve it, and to enjoy it.

SELECTED BIBLIOGRAPHY

This is a selected bibliography, limited to books that were either mentioned in the text and require further identification or that provide more information on subjects covered in the text. No attempt has been made to include any encyclopedias or books in the various specialties. For those, readers should be guided by the suggestions on pages 14 to 18.

Art at Auction: The Year at Sotheby Park Bernet. London: Sotheby Park Bernet, yearly.

Christie's Review of the Season. New York: The Macmillan Company, yearly.

CLARK, KENNETH. *Another Part of the Wood.* New York: Harper & Row, 1974.

Collector's Handbook. Cincinnati, Ohio: Cincinnati Art Museum, 1978.

"Commentary on Personal Property Appraisal" (monograph). Washington, D.C.: American Society of Appraisers, 1976.

CONNOLLY, ROBERT D. *The New Collector's Directory for the 1980s.* San Luis Obispo, Calif.: Padre Productions, 1980.

FRANKLIN, LINDA CAMPBELL. *Antiques and Collectibles: A Bibliography of Works in English.* Metuchen, N.J., and London: Scarecrow Press, Inc., 1978.

KINARD, EPSIE. *The Care and Keeping of Antiques.* New York: Hawthorn Books, 1971.

LEE, RUTH WEBB. *Antique Fakes and Reproductions.* Framingham Centre, Mass.: Ruth Webb Lee, 1938.

LEINWAHL, STANLEY. *So You Think You're Covered?* New York: Charles Scribner's Sons, 1977.

LYNES, RUSSELL. *The Tastemakers.* New York: Harper & Brothers, 1949.

MCGRATH, LEE PARR. *Housekeeping with Antiques.* New York: Dodd, Mead & Co., 1971.

MILLS, JOHN FITZMAURICE. *The Care of Antiques.* London: Arlington Books, 1964.

NUTTING, WALLACE. *Furniture Treasury.* Cambridge, Mass.: Harvard University Press, 1928.

ORMSBEE, THOMAS H. *Care and Repair of Antiques.* New York: Gramercy Publishing Co. (Crown), 1949.

PETERSON, HAROLD L. *How Do You Know It's Old?* New York: Charles Scribner's Sons, 1975.

RIGBY, DOUGLAS, and RIGBY, ELIZABETH. *Lock, Stock and Barrel: The Story of Collecting.* New York: J.B. Lippincott, 1944.

SAARINEN, ALINE B. *The Proud Possessors.* New York: Random House, 1958.

SAVAGE, GEORGE. *Forgeries, Fakes and Reproductions.* New York: Frederick A. Praeger, 1963.

Treasures of America and Where to Find Them. Pleasantville, N.Y.: Reader's Digest, Inc., 1974.

INDEX